RESTORING GRATITUDE

Finding Beauty in a Broken World

Alvin Reid

Be Inspired Books

ISBN-13: 9798552731923

Cover design by: Jacqueline Reid
Library of Congress Control Number: 2018675309
Printed in the United States of America

CONTENTS

INTRODUCTION

Gratitude Is A Guide

"GRATITUDE WILL UNLOCK ALL OTHER VIRTUES." —— KEVIN KELLY[1]

"ENTER HIS GATES WITH THANKSGIVING, AND HIS COURTS WITH PRAISE! GIVE THANKS TO HIM; BLESS HIS NAME! FOR THE LORD IS GOOD; HIS STEADFAST LOVE ENDURES FOREVER, AND HIS FAITHFULNESS TO ALL GENERATIONS." —— PSALM 100:4-5.

I n 1996, Katie found herself stuck in a rut: a joyless job, financial distress, and adrift spiritually. She battled shame and guilt emotionally, living a roller coaster life, surviving each day until the weekend.

As she reflected on all that was missing from her life Katie began thinking about how we respond to gifts. She made a conscious decision to begin expressing gratitude for the gifts of life. She started saying "thank you" for her job, her car, the weather, and in particular, the suffering she faced. "Instead of feeling shame for the mistakes I made, I chose to be grateful for them because of the insight and growth they provided,"[2] she said.

This deliberate practice surprised her: the more she expressed gratitude the more life began to change for the better. She found gratitude to be both a pathway to see life's beauty and an aid in dealing with hard times.

Gratitude does this. The Bible and recent research agree: gratitude is far more powerful than we realize. It is not a magic potion or a cure-all; but it's ability to help us see beauty in a broken world is real.

The regular practice of gratitude changes things: your intimacy with God, your perspective, your response to circumstances both good and bad, and your relationships with others.

You know what it's like to be surprised by joy through the kind actions of another person. You also know how people appreciate it when you express gratitude to them. Gratitude impacts our spiritual life, our emotional and mental wellbeing, and helps us physically and relationally. In particular, it is connected to joy.

I'm building a little cabin in the woods on the family farm where I now live. Just the other day I learned a neighbor was giving away piles of barnwood lumber for free! I hopped in my trusty 1989 Toyota pickup (I call it the Gray Ghost), got two big loads of wood, and sweated about two gallons in the heat loading and unloading it. As I admired the stack of lumber in the barn, my fatigue was overshadowed by the sense of gratitude I had for the unexpected blessing of the lumber.

I think of gratitude as super food for the mind.

But gratitude is more than that. Sure, adding broccoli or avocado or another so-called "super food" is good for your health; you can still have a healthy life without either one of those. But you can't live a fulfilled life if you are an ungrateful person.

Gratitude is a game changer.

Here's some good news: deliberately choosing to practice gratitude can help to retell your current story in a different way, just like Katie's. And it can do so faster than you think. Gratitude can be a guide to help us respond to difficulty, overcome our past, practice humility, and find joy.

In a matter of weeks—faster than you can get your body whipped into prime physical shape through diet and exercise—you can see real change in your perspective on life. You can experience the restorative power of gratitude.

The following eight chapters offer a guide into how gratitude can become a pathway to peace and an onramp to joy. Like a skilled carpenter who takes an abandoned piece of furniture and restores it to its original beauty, you too can begin to see the beauty in our world despite its stains.

I've always tried to be a grateful person. But when I learned I could choose to be grateful regardless of my circumstances or emotional state, I stepped into a world of increasing joy. It has literally changed my life, helping me to fight depression and anxiety, to discover peace, and ultimately, to live with joy. This is a life journey worth taking.

You can, like King David, exclaim,

Bless the Lord, O my soul,
and all that is within me,
bless His holy name! (Psalm 103:1).

Let's get started.

1. GRATEFUL PEOPLE CAN FACE A BROKEN WORLD

"GRATITUDE FOR THE SEEMINGLY INSIGNIFICANT—A SEED—THIS PLANTS THE GIANT MIRACLE." — ANN VOSKAMP[3]

"LIVING IN GRATITUDE IS LIVING IN TRUTH. IT IS THE MOST ACCURATE AND HONEST APPROACH TO LIFE. -- ROBERT EMMONS[4]

"THEN ONE OF THEM, WHEN HE SAW THAT HE WAS HEALED, TURNED BACK, PRAISING GOD WITH A LOUD VOICE; AND HE FELL ON HIS FACE AT JESUS' FEET, GIVING HIM THANKS. NOW HE WAS A SAMARITAN." -- LUKE 17:15-16

K yle Maynard is a best-selling author, ESPY award-winning mixed martial arts athlete, and entrepreneur. His achievements include induction into the National Wrestling Hall of Fame, climbing both Mount Kilimanjaro in Africa and Mount Aconcagua in South America, and building the successful No Excuses Gym.

Kyle is also a quadruple amputee. He accomplished all this without the aid of prosthetics.

Kyle made a choice not to live his life from his limitations; his focus is on thriving. He is a happy person, probably happier than most people who have arms and legs. But he talks more about bliss. His true north for life: "Thinking of what makes me happy doesn't give me the same clarity as thinking about what gives me *bliss*."[5]

When asked about his life and all the challenges he had to overcome, Maynard said, "I am grateful for the moments now of uncertainty and being afraid because I know that all of those moments of growth in my life usually come with a little bit of that uncertainty."[6]

In a world that finds security in certainty, Kyle learned the secret that gratitude is a choice we can all make. If life is more how we respond to circumstances than the circumstances themselves, then living from a posture of gratitude makes a lot of sense.

Being happy is based on circumstances; bliss is a choice.

So is gratitude.

Giving Thanks And Being Grateful

Most of us already choose gratitude each fall in the U.S. On the fourth Thursday each November people—regardless of ethnicity, economic status, political ideology, or religious belief—celebrate Thanksgiving.

What comes to mind when you think of that day? A fresh-baked turkey, homemade pecan pie, family gathering together, or maybe football? As I get older I think more about the nap after the meal! I for one don't think about Black Friday shopping, but if that's you, you be you.

Thanksgiving holiday is good; it's always a good thing to set aside time for family and to give thanks. But this is a book about gratitude's impact on life, not a holiday's impact on our waist.

Giving thanks and being grateful. Same thing, right? They are synonymous in Scripture, but in practical usage today there is a bit of a difference. According to a study at the renowned Wharton School of Business at the University of Pennsylvania, respondents considered "I am grateful" to be more genuine than "Thank you."[7]

Gratitude turns what you have into enough.

A series on gratitude from Michigan State University ob-served: "Gratitude is an emotion expressing an appreciation for what one *has*, as opposed to what one *wants*."[8] We say "thanks" when someone does something for us like holding a door when our hands are full . We instinctively say thanks for gestures like that, sort of like replying "I'm fine," when asked how we are doing whether we're really fine or not. It's almost an auto-response. Throughout this book I will emphasize the word gratitude while also using thanksgiving.

A Gratitude Resurgence

A skilled surfer has no control over the wave she rides, but she knows how to ride it when it crests. Today a wave is rising, bring-ing a focus on gratitude, and it couldn't come soon enough!

I'm writing this in the middle of a global pandemic. We face unrest over social issues and political angst; how does one re-spond to what a friend of mine calls the *Age of Outrage*?[9]

Gratitude is a choice we make to see the blessings we have regardless of the circumstances we face. It doesn't ignore pain; it looks beyond pain to see a bigger picture.

Robert Emmons researches gratitude. "We are at the dawn of a global gratitude renaissance," he writes. "Unprecedented inter-est . . . gratitude is so welcome because this is what gives us the strength of character to make life better not only for ourselves but also for others."[10]

If you are breathing, you have the capacity for gratitude. You don't need a degree in gratitude, amazing people skills, or a higher than average intellect.

I hope this book will lift you up out of the turbulence of life, stand you up on the surfboard, and help you ride the wave of gratitude to a new perspective on life.

It's that important.

You are that important.

Jesus Regards The Grateful

The COVID pandemic introduced us to practices like self-quarantine, social distancing, and wearing masks. This isn't new; medical distancing practices go back at least as far as the book of Leviticus in the Old Testament.

We read in Leviticus 13:45-46 that anyone with leprosy had to follow guidelines far more stringent than wearing a mask and distancing six feet. They were required to tear their clothing to identify their quarantined state. Adding to their indignity, they had to cry out, "Unclean! Unclean!" if anyone came near them.

One day as Jesus walked toward Jerusalem, he encountered ten of these lepers. When they saw Jesus they cried, "Jesus, Master, have mercy on us" (Luke 17:13).

Jesus looked at them. How incredible it is to know that Jesus looks at us, whether diseased, broken, marginalized, sin-wrecked, or poor. He *sees* us.

He sees lepers ostracized from their community and he sees you in your uncertainty.

He told the lepers to go show themselves to the priest. Miraculously, as they simply obeyed Jesus they found themselves healed of their leprosy.

Ten lepers who knew what it meant to be separated, stigmatized, and traumatized by their illness were suddenly healed. That's cause for gratitude!

But one stood out:

Then one of them, when he saw that he was healed, turned back, praising God with a loud voice; and he fell on his face at Jesus' feet, giving him thanks. Now he was a Samaritan. Then Jesus answered, "Were not ten cleansed? Where are the nine? Was no one found to return and give praise to God except this foreigner?" And he said to him, "Rise and go your way; your faith has made you well" (Luke 17:15-19).

Luke carefully noted the grateful leper was a Samaritan, an outcast loathed by the Jews. He who had been yelling "Unclean!" now praised God with greater zeal.

That got the Lord's attention.

Gratitude has a way of doing that.

I doubt you've been healed of leprosy. But if you have been cleansed from the guilt of sin through Jesus Christ, what a cause for daily gratitude! Instead of a skin disease, we all have a sin disease. Rather than being quarantined for 14 days due to possible contamination because of a virus, we are separated from God for all eternity because of sin.

But there is a cure for our malady: we like the lepers can cry "Jesus, have mercy on me!" Because of Jesus' work on the cross we can find forgiveness, cleansing, and a new life. How often do you express gratitude for this wonder? How much more should we "with a loud voice" express our praise and gratitude to God?

If you've never tasted and seen that the Lord is good (Psalm 34:8), you can call on Him today. If you are unclear about this, please go to www.everystudent.com for more help or email me at ALRAdvising@gmail.com.

If you've lost the wonder of salvation, that's a dangerous place to be. I know; I've been there. And if you think it couldn't happen to you, listen to the Word of the Lord to Cain: "Sin is crouching at the door" (Genesis 4:7).

Reminding yourself daily of the joy of salvation is a good start toward a lifestyle of gratitude. Gratitude turns our eyes toward eternity.

It Is That Important

Gratitude and thankfulness show up regularly throughout the Bible. I searched the ESV Bible and found "gratitude" mentioned 45 times; "grateful" 26; "thanks" over 300 times; "thanksgiving" 155. It's prominent in particular in the Psalms and Paul's letters.

"Gratitude is not just good medicine, though, a nice sentiment, a warm fuzzy feeling, or a strategy or tactic for being happier or healthier," says Emmons. *"It is also the truest approach to life.* We did not create or fashion ourselves, and we did not get to where we are in life by ourselves. So living in gratitude is living in truth. It is the most accurate and honest approach to life."[11]

I agree. Gratitude is fundamental to life, not ancillary. It's like the fabric of our clothes, not an add-on accessory; it's as essential to your life as a major organ, not something replaceable like a toenail.

Being a grateful person shapes all facets of life.

The English word *gratitude* comes from the Latin *gratia*, meaning "grace." In the Bible, the grace of God refers to receiving that which we do not deserve, including the forgiveness of sin and the love of God. Gratitude gives us the grace to be patient with others and to forgive.

Gratitude turns what we have into enough.

In 2019, I crossed the 60-year mark, and it looked like nothing I'd envisioned. I'd just walked—or crawled to be more accurate—through a season where I was broken, filled with shame, and found myself on the border of helpless and hopeless. A year prior I saw my world shattered to pieces and I swung the hammer that smashed it.

I've faced things I never expected: failure, divorce, sin, sorrow, and heartache. I spent a month laying on the floor at my mother's home in Alabama weeping daily, crying out to God, and searching the Scriptures.

In the middle of the mess I made, I found grace renewed, and in that grace a perspective on gratitude I'd never had before.

If you've screwed up your life royally; if you find yourself struggling to find peace and joy; or if you think your failure is final, I have good news: if you are breathing, God has more for you. He is here and He is good.

His grace is both amazing and available.

If harsh circumstances stormed through your life like an Oklahoma tornado, there is a way forward. If you battle inner demons, fear the future, or can't seem to escape your own mistakes: there is a path to follow, and it starts with baby steps called gratitude.

When you reach the end of yourself you can either surrender to the God who loves you or keep on trying your way. A loving God's way is the best way.

Gratitude can turn our mourning into laughter, our weeping into singing.

Gratitude can become a lifestyle. I know, because it has become mine, and it has rescued me from the pit of despair, rearranged my priorities, and simplified my life.

I'm grateful for friends who care about who you are more than what you've done. I'm grateful most of all for the grace of God in Jesus Christ. I've taught it and thought I understood it. But I never knew the wonder of grace until I had no other hope. Grace taught me gratitude.

Choosing To Be Grateful In A Broken World

It only takes a brief review of today's headlines or scrolling through social media to realize how broken our world is. Division, unrest, injustice, and fear mark our times. Gratitude helps us to understand what we control and what we don't. There's a lot we can't control:

—Politicians and their (often) empty promises;
—What people post on social media;
—The negative news media;
—People who choose anger, outrage, or fear.

Gratitude is not necessarily our first choice, but it's typically the right choice.

I'm grateful God is in control; I'm grateful pandemics end. I'm grateful a day is coming when people from all tribes, tongues, and nations will worship God together.

I can choose to be grateful rather than angry, kind rather than outraged, and to trust rather than fear.

If you battle with anxiety, depression, or other issues I want to encourage you to have a conversation with a healthcare professional. If you ever think about suicide or how you might take your life, please stop reading and call 1-800-273-8255.

This book can help those who struggle with mental health issues as an encouragement to embrace gratitude, but it is not a replacement for help from a professional. In recent years, a godly, skilled counselor walked with me through a dark season. I know the amazing, real, and lasting impact this can make. There is no shame in getting help. If you can go to a personal trainer to help get more fit, a doctor to get well, or a tutor for help with a subject in school, you can see a counselor to help with emotional and mental struggles.

Gratitude Is Available To All

Gratitude is available it is to anyone who chooses its path. The youth cut from his ball team can choose to be grateful that he has other options in life than one shot at one team. The lady spurned by the man she loves can be grateful that love does not die when a relationship ends.

This book is especially for those who love Jesus Christ but are burned out on some of the forms of Christianity that bear his name today. Let's be real: a lot of people have been hurt by the church. Maybe you stopped attending church the past few years; maybe your recent difficulties have created a burden which makes you question the basic goodness of God. Perhaps you are a person of color who has a lifetime of stories of injustices that few if any in the majority culture seem to understand.

Gratitude has no color barrier. You will find the grateful among both the urban poor and rural farmers, from youth to the elderly.

Gratitude is a choice you and I can make daily.

Putting Gratitude Into Practice

1. Picture a time in the recent past when you faced disappointment or discouragement. How might you find a source of gratitude even though the circumstances don't change?

2. Who is someone you could call, text, email, or visit to tell them how grateful you are for them? When can you act on this?

3. Write down three simple things for which you are grateful. Take time to consider how these bring value to your life.

4. Pray a simple prayer of thanks to God for a specific blessing in your life.

2. GRATEFUL PEOPLE RECOGNIZE THE WONDER OF GRATITUDE

"PIGLET NOTICED THAT EVEN THOUGH HE HAD A VERY SMALL HEART, IT COULD HOLD A RATHER LARGE AMOUNT OF GRATITUDE."— A.A. MILNE, WINNIE THE POOH[12]

"I FEEL ONLY GRATITUDE FOR MY LIFE, FOR EVERY MOMENT I HAVE LIVED. . . . NEVER ONCE IN MY LIFE DID I ASK GOD FOR SUCCESS . . . I ASKED FOR WONDER, AND HE GAVE IT TO ME." –– RABBI ABRAHAM HESCHEL[13]

"MY SOUL MAGNIFIES THE LORD, AND MY SPIRIT REJOICES IN GOD MY SAVIOR, FOR HE HAS LOOKED ON THE HUMBLE ESTATE OF HIS SERVANT." –– MARY, THE MOTHER OF JESUS, LUKE 1:47

I'm old enough to remember when phones were attached to the wall (think Napoleon Dynamite?). It was a big deal when phones went cordless. Then, along came these big, angular, awkward things called a cellular phone. They became available to the public in 1984; I got my first in the mid-1990s. It would not fit in your back pocket then.

Eventually we added texting. The first text, "Merry Christmas"––just words, no emojis––was sent December 3, 1992.

The iPhone made its debut to the public June 29, 2007. The revolution had begun. It's hard to imagine life without one now. Today there are more cell phones on earth than people.

What are your most useful apps? Google Maps for me! What are your favorites apps? A game? Social media? The smartphone has revolutionized communication, although it hasn't helped us with relationships very much.

If your life were a smartphone it would be easy to think of gratitude as one of a thousand apps you might use occasionally. Instead, think of it as the screen on your smartphone. If you've ever had a badly cracked screen you know how distracting it can be. The phone still works, but things aren't as clear as it should be. It's annoying, right?

Our lives are cracked. There are so many issues ranging from a major crisis to everyday distractions that can sap our energy and rob us of joy. Looking at life through the lens of gratitude, like seeing through a clear screen, can affect your perspective on everything.

We could use a clean screen.

We Are Drawn To Wonder

When you are stressed and want to get away where do you go? Or, if you could go anywhere, where would that be? Most people say somewhere outdoors: the mountains, the ocean, a lake, or the woods. There's a reason we name places like the Grand Canyon a national park.

Why is that? Two reasons, really. First, we are drawn to *wonder*.

We love wonderful things: nature, a great book or movie, a fine meal, or a special relationship. God put that in us when He made us in His image (Genesis 1:26-27).

But there is a second reason: we want to escape *worry*. Right now, what cares are on your mind? We like to take vacations to beautiful places to capture some wonder in the middle of our worry.

We live between the tension of two things:

Embracing   Escaping
Wonder———————————————————Worry

Wonder feeds *excitement*; *worry* drains us *emotionally*.

Here's the problem: Seeking wonder on our own leads us to crave one experience after another, the next one better than the last. Worry tempts us to build our life on escaping our problems rather than facing them.

Wonder can lead to addictions aimed at giving us the next dose of excitement: porn, bad relationships, or consumerism (let me buy the next wonderful thing). Worry can lead us to seek escape from life's stresses, leading to alcoholism, narcissism, and other ills.

Wonder draws us to *beauty;* worry reveals our *brokenness.* Wonder ignites *passion;* worry amplifies *pain.*

What if I told you both the destination to our search for *wonder* and the solution to the *worry* we experience is found in the Story God is telling? In the middle of our search is **worship.**

Embracing   WORSHIP   Escaping
Wonder———————————————————Worry

This is why the good news in Jesus is such good news. When we understand it, we experience *wonder* as we know and love our God through *worship*, through the One who made us and saves us.

Augustine said it in a prayer: "You have made us, O God, and our hearts are restless till they find rest in you.

Working through the pain of my own brokenness I've learned

the simple wonder of sitting at the edge of the forest at the family farm to watch and hear God's amazing creation. As I write this the tomatoes, zucchini, and peppers are growing just fine. The petunias are blooming, and the birds cover their feeders. Calves run across the pasture without a care.

I experienced something recently that you might rate somewhere between "gross" and "no thank you" but I consider wonderful. I'm talking about a gorgeous gray rat snake I recently encountered on the farm. I picked it up, about five feet in length. It was quite docile, but I'm really comfortable around reptiles. I made a video (of course) and released it in the barn so it could chase rats.

What does this have to do with gratitude? Most of us find some type of animal to be wonderful. For me, it's reptiles. There is something fascinating, even wonderful to me about an animal that strikes fear in so many. When I experience wonderful things—whether in creation, in answered prayer, or in an unexpected blessing—gratitude springs forth from my heart, turning my attention to worshiping a good, generous, and gracious God.

Simple Steps To Wonder

How do we experience moments of wonder in a world so filled with distractions? *First, we can cherish past moments of wonder.* I often reflect on the beauty and wonder of creation; it inspires me to worship the God who made it all. I can also remember some wonderful memories from the past: the birth of a child, writing that first book, or a memorable trip overseas.

Second, we can also develop the habit of recognizing blessings as they come in the present. It's so easy to take things for granted, isn't it? It's easy for me to get frustrated when there's a line at the checkout at the grocery store, but do I pause to give thanks when there is no line? I have a friend who has difficult memories from childhood because her father complained in anger whenever he paid the bills. I want to be grateful I have the ability to pay my bills when they come. Gratitude is often the entryway for worship in my life.

Third, we can look to the future with gratitude. I'm confident in a God who loves me and is for me, so I don't look to the future with apprehension. I don't base my life on what is broken in our world or in my life or on what other broken people think. Life has been tough at times and I've screwed up plenty, but I am grateful daily for the promise of the day ahead. I find God's Word reminding me that failure isn't final, and I can see the future expectantly.

A Mindfulness Of Gratitude

Tracy DiNunzio, founder and CEO of Tradesy, was born with spina bifida. She underwent numerous surgeries throughout her childhood. Reflecting on how she's learned to respond to the difficulties she has faced in life, she said: "If you spend your time focusing on the things that are wrong, and that's what you express and project to people you know, you don't become a source of growth for people, you become a source of destruction for people. That draws more destructiveness."[14]

Tracy decided at one point to go on a "complaining diet," where she chose not to think about her pain or to think negatively about her circumstances. "It took a long time and I wasn't perfect at it," she found, "[but] replacing those thoughts helped me start moving my life in a better direction, where I wasn't obsessing about what was wrong." [15]

Try to respond to every instance of wonder and every personal challenge by finding gratitude in the middle of it. Turn your wonder into worship toward God. Turn your worry over life's challenges to pursue God in worship. You can even be grateful when you fail at this and give in to complaining and worry, because God's love is not conditioned by your performance. It's not always easy, and it's ok to say that sometimes life kinda sucks, and you don't always respond as you should.

What if your personal culture, or your operating system responded with gratitude, joy, and kindness as a default? Sure, we all have our moments. We are human. But don't you enjoy spending time with someone who defaults to giving versus someone who flips to taking, whining, or demeaning others by gaslighting them?

Mary's Wonder At The Choice Of God

Mary was young when the angel of the Lord appeared to her as recorded in Luke 1, "Greetings, O favored one, the Lord is with you!" (Luke 1:28) the angel said. Seeing Mary's consternation, the angel continued, "Do not be afraid, Mary, for you have found favor with God. And behold, you will conceive in your womb and bear a son, and you shall call his name Jesus" (Luke 1:30-31). She replied with understandable skepticism: "How will this be, since I am a virgin?" (Luke 1:34).

The angel declared: "The Holy Spirit will come upon you, and the power of the Most High will overshadow you; therefore the child to be born will be called holy—the Son of God" (Luke 1:35). Imagine being a poor Jewish girl living on the fringe of the Roman Empire, betrothed to a carpenter named Joseph, and being told you will bear the Son of God who will take away the world's sin.

Mary hurried to see her relative Elizabeth, who had been barren but was to give birth to John the Baptist in her old age. God, the creator of the heavens and the earth, entrusted the hope of humanity to a young virgin and the herald of His coming to a barren, elderly woman. His ways are not our ways.

Filled with wonder and gratitude, Mary gave the *Magnificat*, her song to the Lord, which gushes with gratitude and praise:

My soul magnifies the Lord, and my spirit rejoices in God my Savior, for he has looked on the humble estate of His servant. For behold, from now on all generations will call me blessed; for he who is mighty has done great things for me, and holy is his name.

And his mercy is for those who fear him from generation to generation. He has shown strength with his arm; he has scattered the proud in the thoughts of their hearts; he has brought down the mighty from their thrones and exalted those of humble estate; he has filled the hungry with good things, and the rich he has sent away empty.

He has helped his servant Israel, in remembrance of his mercy, as he spoke to our fathers, to Abraham and to his offspring forever (Luke 1:46-55).

Wonder toward God brings gratitude which in turn breaks forth in worship and relieves our worry.

A Threat To Our Lifestyle Is Not A Threat To Our Lives

It's hard to see the wonder in life when our world is falling apart. Gratitude can help with perspective about life, even when it stinks sometimes. I just saw a news article about a lady complaining that her granddad only gave her $4,000 for her wedding dress. That's not a real problem.

When you've lost your job and you have to make a decision about cutting the cable so you can keep your electricity, it's uncomfortable, but it's not life-threatening. But choosing between paying the rent and feeding your children is a real problem because it effects both your shelter and your sustenance. In 2019, I worked all that year at a medical supply company. I saw so many people who were on fixed incomes. Seeing them labor over whether to spend $24 on a copay for a walker they really needed to ambulate, or watching dear people struggle to breathe through the cannula providing oxygen to their lungs gave me a much-needed perspective on life.

I always told my children never to say they were "starving" when they were hungry because they were never going to starve, and I'd been places in the world where people do face starvation. But I have pretty much had all I needed all my life. My income the past two years dropped dramatically, but so did my needs.

I have a new perspective on life for which I'm grateful. You see, in prosperous America we easily confuse stress on our **lifestyle** with stress on *life* itself. Stress about losing your position at work is real, but it is not a life or death proposition; it does impact your lifestyle. In a land of material abundance we can confuse what we really need with what we greedily covet.

Gratitude helps us focus on the minimum required for our life, not the maximum we want for a lifestyle.

I've been so low I wanted to die. But I didn't die. And the lessons learned since bottoming out have helped me distinguish between a lifestyle of affluence and a lifestyle of significance. I learned this the hard way. I went from financial prosperity to extreme scarcity; I also went from popular to puny, from respected to repulsive. One day I will write more about this, but for now, I will say I screwed up and wound up on my face, starting life over, depressed and in despair.

But I didn't stay in the pit. And I didn't lose everything. The Lord never left me, and I continually ran to Him. I still do today.

One of the first passages the Lord gave me was Psalm 40, which I put on the dash of my vehicle and memorized:

I waited patiently for the Lord;
  he inclined to me and heard my cry.
He drew me up from the pit of destruction,
  out of the miry bog,
and set my feet upon a rock,
  making my steps secure.

He put a new song in my mouth,
  a song of praise to our God.
Many will see and fear,
  and put their trust in the Lord.

It took time, but after a season of seclusion, lament, counseling, and repentance, I began to see things through the lens of gratitude. "God's not done with you," a former colleague reminded me. "Your best days are ahead," a pastor from years back encouraged me.

I became grateful for the opportunity to drive a truck for an auto parts dealer for a season. It taught me new things, allowed me to meet new friends, and paid the bills. It also gave me hours a day alone in the truck to weep before the Lord, give thanks for his kindness, and to listen to Scripture, worship music, and messages.

If your life is hunky-dory; if you have never walked through a season of brokenness—whether of your own doing, because of others hurting you, or simply because we live in a sin-stained, wrecked world—you may not appreciate the value of gratitude.

Or, if your surface spirituality covers up the pain that's real inside you, perhaps you haven't yet reached the place of brokenness to latch on to gratitude. The more honest we are with God, the more real He is to us, and gratitude helps us to assess ourselves honestly.

I learned that if you change your ends, your means aren't so demanding. I'm thankful to learn how often in my life I stressed over *lifestyle* issues as if they were essential to life itself.

I've found wonder in a minimalist lifestyle. No, I don't live in a home with one chair, one plate, and a single fork. I have more than I need, but I have far less than I once enjoyed. Except now I realize I wasn't enjoying it.

As Paul wrote:

But godliness with contentment is great gain, for we brought nothing into the world, and we cannot take anything out of the world. But if we have food and clothing, with these we will be content. (1 Timothy 6:6-8).

I looked through the cracks in my broken world to see the face of a gracious God, and I am grateful. You can see beauty in the brokenness the same way and look through the eyes of wonder to experience true worship.

Putting Gratitude Into Practice

1. Every morning for the next few weeks, look in the mirror in the morning and say, "I'm grateful for another great day to live and to love." (Put a stick-it note up on the mirror if you need a reminder).

2. Look for little things you are thankful for throughout your day: your car cranked just fine; you had food to eat; you can walk, or hear, or feel the warmth of the sun.

3. Remember things that filled you with wonder when you were a child. Make a list of some of those. Take time to be grateful for the childlike wonder these evoke.

3. GRATEFUL PEOPLE LEARN THE BENEFITS OF GRATITUDE

"WHEN WE GIVE CHEERFULLY AND ACCEPT GRATEFULLY, EVERYONE IS BLESSED."— MAYA ANGELOU[16]

"THE STRUGGLE ENDS WHEN THE GRATITUDE BEGINS." –– NEALE DONALD WALSH[17]

"GIVE THANKS IN ALL CIRCUMSTANCES; FOR THIS IS THE WILL OF GOD IN CHRIST JESUS FOR YOU." –– THE APOSTLE PAUL, 1 THESSALONIANS 5:18.

What do you do in response to an unexpected and genuinely helpful gift? Brennan Manning tells the story of speaking at a church in Louisiana when a stranger approached him afterward. "I've prayed about this," the man muttered, sliding an envelope into Manning's pocket.

Later that evening Manning opened the envelope. It contained a check for six thousand dollars. He immediately thought of a man he'd met on a recent visit to work among the poor living in a garbage dump in Juarez, Mexico. The man had ten children, three of whom had died from the oppressive poverty there. He sent the check to the father.

What did the father do? He wrote Brennan nine letters in two days, letters filled with gratitude, letters describing how he was using the money for his family and others he knew. Manning commented about what this shows about someone who understands their poverty:

> When he receives a gift he first experiences, [he] then expresses genuine gratitude. Having nothing, he appreciates the slightest gift. I have been given the utterly undeserved gift of salvation in Jesus Christ. Through no merit of mine, I have been given a bona fide invitation to drink new wine forever at the wedding feast in the kingdom of God.[18]

The benefits of gratitude are many and have the capacity to reshape our vision of the world.

The Performance-Enhancing Role Of Gratitude

Emmons reports how collective studies on the subject across disciplines reveals how gratitude's impact on "individual and collective flourishing is becoming more and more apparent."[19] He gives two reasons. First, the fact that gratitude enhances the everyday lives of people is both quantifiable and sustainable. Second, practicing gratitude is readily accessible to anyone: "You are never too old, too young, too rich, too poor, to live gratefully."[20]

This applies to all areas of life. Calling it the "Ultimate Performance-Enhancing Substance," Emmons adds, "Unlike other performance-enhancers, gratitude is always legal, has no side effects, and you cannot overdose on it. Gratitude improves performance in every domain of life that has been studied."[21] I want to show you specific areas where gratitude affects us.

Mental And Emotional Benefits Of Gratitude

We can by deliberate practice bring about a change emotionally. As Achor puts it, "When our brains constantly scan for and

focus on the positive, we profit from three of the most important tools available to us: happiness, gratitude, and optimism." He
then describes the specific impact of gratitude on our emotions:
"Countless other studies have shown that consistently grateful
people are more energetic, emotionally intelligent, forgiving,
and less likely to be depressed, anxious, or lonely. And it's not
that people are only grateful because they are happier, either;
gratitude has proven to be a significant cause of positive out-
comes."[22]

One 2018 study found that intentionally practicing gratitude
causes:[23]

—Increased happiness and positive mood
—More satisfaction with life
—Less materialistic leanings
—Less likely to experience burnout

Gratitude helps those who struggle with mental health issues.
One study examined almost 300 adults seeking mental health
counseling at a university. These adults also displayed lower than
average levels of mental health.

Subjects were put in three groups.

—The first group wrote a letter of gratitude weekly for three
weeks.

—The second group wrote down their thoughts and feelings
about negative experiences.

—The third group did nothing.

In addition, counseling services were made available to all
three groups. Researchers found that in weeks four and 12, Group
One showed significantly improved mental health. They also
found that when counseling is paired with gratitude, it brings
more benefits than counseling alone, as vital as that is.

They offered four insights gleaned from the study:[24]

1. Gratitude unshackles us from toxic emotions. It seems that "gratitude letter writing produces better mental health by shifting one's attention away from toxic emotions, such as resentment and envy. When you write about how grateful you are to others and how much other people have blessed your life, it might become considerably harder for you to ruminate on your negative experiences."

2. Gratitude helps even if you don't share it. The group who wrote letters weren't required to send them; only 23 percent did. But those who didn't send the letters experienced the same benefit as those who did: "The mere act of writing the letter can help you appreciate the people in your life and shift your focus away from negative feelings and thoughts."

3. Gratitude's benefits take time. For emotional health to be impacted by gratitude we need to give it time: "Although the different groups in our study did not differ in mental health levels one week after the end of the writing activities, individuals in the gratitude group reported better mental health than the others four weeks after the writing activities, and this difference in mental health became even larger 12 weeks after the writing activities."

4. Gratitude has lasting effects on the brain. Three months after the study the researchers took some of those who wrote letters to study any ongoing impact:

> *We found that across the participants, when people felt more grateful, their brain activity was distinct from brain activity related to guilt and the desire to help a cause. . . . This suggests that people who are more grateful are also more attentive to how they express gratitude.*

Researchers found expressing gratitude aids with suicidal patients. Suicidal inpatients writing gratitude letters reported an 88 percent reduction in a sense of hopelessness.[25]

Gratitude also helps to deal with a crisis. A study of health-care workers during the height of the pandemic discovered that those who kept a gratitude journal for two weeks "Produced sustained reductions in perceived stress (28 per cent) and depression (16 per cent)."[26] Gratitude has also been shown to reduce levels of the stress hormone cortisol 23 percent and decrease dietary fat intake by 25 per cent when people keep a journal.

Physical Benefits Of Gratitude

I enjoy reading and learning about health and fitness. I'm not an expert though I've learned a lot. For instance, if you are unhealthy and want to embrace a healthier lifestyle the first step is not to start tracking your macros with your diet or hitting the gym to exercise. The first step is to ensure you are getting enough sleep. According to the CDC one in three Americans don't get enough sleep. After that, drink enough water, because we are also dehydrated as a population.

Taking time before bed to reflect with gratitude for your day and for your life is a proven way to help you sleep better. Studies show gratitude journaling in particular helps us physically in other ways as well:[27]

—Stronger immune systems
—Less bothered by aches and pains
—Lower blood pressure
—Exercise more and take better care of their health
—Sleep longer and feel more refreshed upon waking

I know personally by starting each day with gratitude helps to motivate me to take better care of myself and my health.

Relationship Benefits Of Gratitude

I will talk more about relationships and gratitude in the next chapter but wanted to note its impact here. Researchers found the practice of gratitude journaling brought a number of relational benefits. People are:[28]

—More helpful, generous, and compassionate
—More forgiving
—More outgoing
—Less likely to feel lonely and isolated

People who express gratitude tend to reflect more on relationships and their value. When intentional acts of gratitude are practiced (remembering a grateful experience, writing a letter, and so on), people doing so have a greater sense of connectedness to others.

One study will be especially encouraging to parents and teachers. A study of a group of 9th and 10th grade students discovered those who expressed gratitude to parents, teachers, or coaches felt more closely related to them and felt more confident and competent.[29]

I saw this personally in the life of a night grader I tutored for a year I will call Eddie. Eddie was an at-risk student. I knew an associate principal at my daughter's high school and offered to help Eddie. It was awkward the first day we met; I was a middle-aged white guy; he was an African American young man who wasn't excited initially about our meeting. I've always loved young people and sought to encourage them, and we both warmed up to our weekly meetings at lunch on Wednesdays. I helped him with history, English, and other topics. I wasn't a lot of help with math I confess, but I did something more for him.

I encouraged Eddie to thank his teachers for their patience with him and for any help they could give as he sought to renew his academic performance. He was a bright young man who had simply come from a difficult home situation. He went from failing all his classes to passing them and moving on to the next grade. But what blessed me as well was the response of the teachers in the emails sent to me. They said less about his academic performance than his disposition. He proved himself a conscientious, competent, and increasingly confident young man. Having him express gratitude regularly to his teachers (and to his mom, which I encouraged as well) impacted both Eddie and others.

Spiritual Benefits Of Gratitude

Gratitude brings us to a more God-centered place as we realize what James says: "Every good gift and every perfect gift is from above, coming down from the Father of lights" (James 1:17). Because God is God and God is good, we can trust Him.

Being honest with yourself about things you struggle with is critical to spiritual growth. No matter how "mild" your inner battles may seem, it's vital to address them. It's too easy to give the veneer of "everything is fine" when you aren't actually fine. Lots of people carry that facade every day.

Honestly admitting a struggle, whether depression, anxiety, worry over the past or cares about the future, followed by turning to Scripture, has an amazing capacity to set things in a better place. It's like repotting a plant from a small pot to one with more space, from dry clay to fresh dirt.

Gratitude grows from such soil, feeding the parched roots. A godly friend or counselor who walks with you is like fertilizer, giving more strength. We weren't made to walk this road alone; we all need others. Admitting that is a sign of strength, not weakness.

We aren't superheroes. We are broken people with no hope if not for a merciful Savior. Christ came to give us real life: "For while we were still weak, at the right time Christ died for the ungodly" (Romans 5:6).

Christ is enough. Let that reality be at the core of your spiritual life.

And for that truth we can be grateful.

In my late 30s I broke my hip. Long story, but let's just say I have a tendency to be very rough on myself including physically. I got an artificial hip replacement at age 38, which will ruin your whole day. One day as I recovered at home it hit me: as I saw my son dressed in his soccer gear and heading off to his game, I knew the hip replacement meant a lot of things I planned with my kids, from wrestling matches to tackle football games, were not going to be the same.

I suddenly, uncontrollably began to weep. I just lost it. All I could see was what I had lost because of the surgery. If you're mad at God, you might as well tell Him; He already knows! So, I told God I was angry for my plight.

Suddenly. I pictured in my mind's eye a specific verse from the Bible.

It was 1 Thessalonians 5:18: "Give thanks in all circumstances; for this is the will of God in Christ Jesus for you."

That verse came to me as I sat in my tears of self-pity. It is the will of God to give thanks. That's not so hard; it's easy to be grateful when thinking of all of His blessings.

But that's not exactly what the verse says. Give thanks "in all circumstances." Not *because* of them, but *in* them; in the middle of difficult times we can yet give thanks.

When you get an artificial hip in the prime of life, give thanks.

When the dream promotion was given to someone else, give thanks.

When you get the divorce papers, give thanks.

When the doctor says, "It's cancer," give thanks.

When you are mistreated because you are different, give thanks.

This is not easy. It's not something you can do on your own. Nor can you do what Paul said in the verse just before verse 18: "Rejoice always, pray without ceasing" (1 Thessalonians 5:16-17). When we lean into our pain, asking God to stir in us gratitude when it's not natural to do so, we can see God clearly even when our world is foggy.

As I sat there in tears thinking of what I had lost because of an artificial hip, I confessed my sin. "God," I prayed, "I am honestly not thankful right now."

As soon as I said that irreverent but honest prayer, my perspective changed. I immediately began to think, "Wait, I can whine like a mule about what I've lost with my kids, or I can focus on what I can do with them." Such a simple pivot. In the years to come I would coach several sports teams and eventually be (in the words of one child) "the loudest freak in the stands" cheering for their team. I became grateful that I lived in a time when artificial hip replacement was possible; 100 years earlier I would have died a painful, slow death in my 30s.

Gratitude refocuses our mind off of our situation and upward to a gracious God.

As I reflected on that day, I realized the importance of pivoting to gratitude whenever possible. This is spiritual work. I try to respond now with curiosity: why am I responding this way? Why is this (circumstance, event, person, etc.) causing this (anxiety, anger, doubt, etc.)? And then I ask, how can I pivot to gratitude?

Gratitude has been critical for my spiritual growth. My faith in Christ and consistent reading of Scripture have been constants whatever storm I face. This is why I start my day, before opening the Word and as my first prayer, writing three things I'm grateful for to the One worthy of unending thanks.

Putting Gratitude Into Practice

1. Take an inventory (or ask someone close to you to do it for you) of the kind of words you use frequently. Grateful people use words like gifts, giving, blessings, blessed, fortunate, abundance, and thankful. Less grateful people tend to talk about problems, burdens, complaints, things they consider unfair to them, or sorrows. Seek to incorporate more grateful terms in your daily conversations.

2. As in a study noted above, write one letter per week for the next three weeks to someone expressing gratitude to them.

3. Take time to remember a specific moment when something wonderful happened. Maybe an answered prayer, a new opportunity, or a special friendship.

4. GRATEFUL PEOPLE VALUE COMMUNITY WITH THE GRATEFUL

"ALWAYS REMEMBER PEOPLE WHO HAVE HELPED YOU ALONG THE WAY, AND DON'T FORGET TO LIFT SOMEONE UP."— ROY T. BENNETT[30]

"GRATITUDE CHANGES THE PANGS OF MEMORY INTO A TRANQUIL JOY." –– DIETRICH BONHOEFFER[31]

AND THEY SANG RESPONSIVELY, PRAISING AND GIVING THANKS TO THE LORD, 'FOR HE IS GOOD, FOR HIS STEADFAST LOVE ENDURES FOREVER TOWARD ISRAEL.' AND ALL THE PEOPLE SHOUTED WITH A GREAT SHOUT WHEN THEY PRAISED THE LORD, BECAUSE THE FOUNDATION OF THE HOUSE OF THE LORD WAS LAID." –– EZRA 3:11

Saman (Iran), Noor (Iraq), and Rachaeal (Nigeria) live in some of the harshest places on earth for Christians. They have each experienced things for their faith most of us in the West never will.

They each show how gratitude can bring encouragement when facing brutal persecution for their faith. As the Open Doors ministry reported, believers in such places "can teach us what gratitude truly looks like––and why it's so important in our lives as we mature in Christ."[32]

Saman, who now lives in Turkey, was a house church leader in Iran. As he met with other believers, he said, "I am encouraged and thank God that you visit us, that my story is shared, and that people pray for me. You can't imagine how much it means to me to know that I am not alone in this." Gratitude is wonderful, but even better when shared in community.

Noor fled Iraq when ISIS invaded. She later returned to rebuild both her own life and her community. She expressed gratitude for the prayers of people she will never meet: "We are grateful that you are helping us, also with your prayers."

Rachaeal John was one of 34 Christian women rescued from Boko Haram. She spent seven months in captivity. She was grateful for the prayers for her rescue: "I wish my eyes could see the people who sent this support to me. I don't know what to say. One thing I will never forget about this gift is that I have brothers and sisters who care for me and who prayed for my rescue."

We were created to know and worship God, but we were also created to be in community with others.

Being with a grateful community multiplies our joy.

Fireflies And Fellowship

As a boy, I was so skinny I had to run around in the shower to get wet! But I was full of energy and loved the outdoors. I loved catching a bunch of lightning bugs (we called them "fireflies"), putting them in a jar, and watching them glow as it got pitch dark. I didn't know the male bugs lit up to attract females; I just thought they were cool.

A biologist in southeast Asia was doing some research in the wetlands among the mango trees. As he looked across the river, he saw trees light up like lightning. Entire trees glowed, then suddenly went dark. He discovered it was caused by a huge swarm of lightning bugs.

Biologists back in the US didn't believe his report. If the male bugs who lit up did so in unison, they reasoned, it would decrease their odds to attract a female. The journal *Science* reported further findings on this peculiar practice: random male bugs lighting up had a 3 percent chance of a female response, but when they all lit up together, the odds went to 82 percent. By connecting with others to light up the sky, their odds of mating and survival increase dramatically.[33]

In our time of radical individualism and self-sufficiency, there is a lesson to be learned from the lightning bugs. Instead of competing with each other, comparing with others, or tearing down those with whom we disagree, what if we gave ourselves to being grateful and to uniting with others who display a grateful heart?

It's An Ugly World Out There—— We Need Each Other

There's a lot in the world to rob us of a grateful life. Rainn Wilson, aka Dwight Schrute from *The Office* quipped, "Cynicism is a disease that robs people of the gift of life."[34] Does it ever seem to you like people are getting meaner? I worked in customer service for a while in the medical supply field. Every person who came to see us was sick, afraid, or angry at their doctor, but decided to take it out on us.

While every now and then someone would get on my last nerve, I mostly welcomed the opportunity to love and care for these dear people. I believe what Alain de Botton stated: "When people seem like they are mean, they're almost never mean. They're anxious."[35]

When the world rubs us the wrong way it's easy to hitch our

lives to the complain-train. Stephen Hawking, the brilliant physicist who suffered for years with ALS before his death in 2018, said, "When you complain, nobody wants to help you."[36]

Complaining is unbecoming, unhelpful, and unnecessary. Mark Twain put it this way, "I am an old man and I have known a great many troubles, but most of them never happened."[37] Or, as the philosopher Seneca put it, "He who suffers before it is necessary suffers more than is necessary."[38]

How do we keep from going down a rat hole of negativity, pessimism, and worst-case-scenario thinking? It's easy to do in our broken world. Being in a community of people who care for you, encourage you, and challenge you to grow helps to break us out of any funk we find ourselves in.

Pastor Chris Hodges of Church of the Highlands in Alabama described one of the small groups in the church. A man discovered he had cancer. As he began chemo and his hair started falling out PC (Pastor Chris) said he noticed one Sunday his whole small group sitting with him in the service. Everyone in the group had either shaved or significantly trimmed their hair. They walked with him the entire journey. Such care evokes a response of gratitude.

I love what C.S. Lewis said: "Friendship is born at the moment when one person says to another: 'What? You too? I thought I was the only one.'"[39] Whatever you face, you aren't the only one.

A Community Of The Grateful

Like all of us, God's people in the Old Testament had a tendency to wander away from their God. Judgment at the hands of the Assyrians brought ruin to the Northern Kingdom of Israel, and the Babylonians later brought the same fate to the Southern Kingdom of Judah. After years of exile, God in His grace let the people begin returning to their land. Though they found Jerusalem in ruins, the early exiles sang a song of gratitude when they returned:

When the Lord restored the fortunes of Zion, we were like those who dream.
Then our mouth was filled with laughter,
and our tongue with shouts of joy;
then they said among the nations,
'The Lord has done great things for them.'
The Lord has done great things for us;
we are glad" (Psalm 126:1-3).

Later as more returned, the rebuilding came under Nehemiah and Ezra. After years of struggle, hardship, and persecution, the temple foundation was completed. The priests and Levites led in a time of worship and thanks:

And they sang responsively, praising and giving thanks to the Lord 'For he is good,
for his steadfast love endures forever toward Israel.'
And all the people shouted with a great shout when they praised the Lord, because the foundation of the house of the Lord was laid (Ezra 3:11).

If there is anything better than giving thanks to God, it is giving thanks to God together in gathered worship with the people of God. This is why so many of the Psalms expressed gratitude and praise. The people of God are at our best when we focus on those things for which we can all thank God.

Paul Tripp describes the connection between corporate worship weekly and the response of thanks. "Corporate worship is designed to make you thankful, not just for possessions and accomplishments, but for what you've been given in Christ." He adds how worshipping together keeps us from the far-too-easy habit of forgetfulness:

Forgetfulness seems like a minor thing. We forget little things every day. We get frustrated for a moment, then remember what we forgot, laugh it off, and go on our way. But forgetfulness is not a minor thing when it comes to grace. It robs you of worship, identity, humility, courage, and hope. Thank God he ordained for us to gather and remember.[40]

Gratitude In Groups

Who is in your world right now who encourages you? Who are the grateful people in your world? Who can you encourage to focus their attention on life's blessings?

"The secret to change and growth is not willpower," Neil Straus observed, "but positive community."[41] That is the genius behind the growth of Crossfit boxes around the world; they are built on community. We need people in our lives who help us see the blessings of life, especially in seasons of pain and brokenness.

The way we act toward one another makes a difference. In 1971, Dr. Phil Zimbardo gave a group of Stanford students specific roles as either "inmates" or "guards" for a study. In a matter of only days, something fascinating happened. The students assigned as guards became increasingly cruel toward the students who were the inmates. But the students who role played as prisoners also began to exhibit significant stress and depression.

These were bright, normal students at a university with impressive academic credentials. Yet they changed their behavior dramatically because of the roles they were given. This demonstrates the impact of being with a group that believes certain things about themselves even when the truth is something else. [42]

The secret to change and growth is not willpower, but positive community. --Neil Strauss

When we are surrounded by people who constantly see the worst in society, the worst in people, rarely show grace, and who are quick to judge, those beliefs and actions can rub off. But the inverse is true as well.

A study by Emmons and Mishra (2011) concluded that there is "considerable evidence that gratitude builds social resources by strengthening relationships."[43] Gratitude:

--Increases prosocial behaviors
--Strengthens relationships
--May help employees' effectiveness
--May increase job satisfaction

The Illusion Of Control

Americans have this radical commitment to freedom expressed in our individualism which brings unintended consequences. We can think of ourselves as autonomous and in control when we really aren't. We can pride ourselves in our supposed self-sufficiency when it actually exposes how fragile we are. Matt Ridley, author of *The Rational Optimist*, observes: "Self-sufficiency is another word for poverty."[44] We need each other.

Mathematician Marcial Losada and UNC psychologist Barbara Frederickson found what's now called the *Losada line*: The sum of the positivity in a system divided by the sum of its negativity. If you have the same number of negative thoughts as positive, you aren't likely to be flourishing. In fact, Frederickson found 3:1 (3 positive thoughts for every negative thought) was the critical mark: "When people have three positive thoughts to every negative thought, they are more optimistic, are happier, and feel more fulfilled."[45] Further, they found that a person who had the same number of positive and negative thoughts displayed depression.

Our sinful and broken world pulls us toward negativity. That's why an alarming number of Christ-followers seem to whine and display outrage online more than gratitude and grace. We have to consciously, intentionally choose worship rather than worry, praise over pain, and gratitude over griping. Imagine the difference in your workplace, neighborhood, family, or your church if people chose to express gratitude just one time more daily.

Ann Voskamp in *The Broken Way* speaks honestly about the real pain of brokenness. Yet her book is also filled with gratitude and hope as it looks to Christ's redemption. "When you feel a radical gratitude for what you have, you end up wanting to go to radical lengths to share it," she writes. "When you are radically grateful for being blessed, you want to be radically generous to the oppressed. Because you know that is the way to radical abundance—there's always more for more to share the grace."[46]

Having A Special Someone

As I approached my 60th birthday I got really interested in health and fitness for more mature folks like me. I didn't believe crossing 60 meant putting one foot in the grave! I found a delightful book called *Younger Next Year* and enjoyed it so much I've read it twice. The book is by a medical doctor named Henry S. Lodge and a humorous former lawyer named Chris Crowley. The authors argue that it's nonsense to think you can't be quite healthy until you reach octogenarian status. Dr. Lodge gives the science and Crowley uses himself (he was well into his 70s when they wrote it) as a guinea pig.

They unpack Seven Rules in great detail, but really focus on two basic ideas: *don't eat crap and get moving* (exercise six days a week). But there is another matter they highlight at the very beginning and again near the end that is critical. The final rule they give, Number Seven, is *connect and commit*. This includes giving of yourself to help and serve others, and being in real, intimate relationships. Near the book's end, they recognize something beyond diet and exercise we must have:

Happiness comes primarily from connection, from giving and getting love and friendship, and that's hard, though

deeply satisfying work. Connect and commit, in other words,
to generate positive emotions and drive away despair.[47]

More than a few find community through interests via Meetup or similar platforms. Small groups at church provide this wonderfully. And, I have men in my life I talk with regularly who challenge and encourage me. But if possible, having a special someone matters as well. If you're married, that should be your spouse. Taking time with your husband or wife to recount things for which you are grateful helps you individually and as a couple. If you aren't, finding that wingman or BFF who shares gratitude with you is crucial.

Studies show gratitude can specifically improve relationships between couples. One study showed when an individual took time to express gratitude for his or her spouse or significant other, the result was not only a more positive feeling for the other person, but a greater willingness then to express concerns to help their relationship grow. In other words, gratitude can open the door for better communication.[48]

Chris Crowly mentioned above also co-wrote *Thinner Next Year* where he talked about being in a marriage, then being stupid. And now, in his second marriage, he is "hanging on tight, by heaven, to a great marriage I don't begin to deserve."[49]

Being divorced is not something I ever thought I would put beside my name. But that is reality; it's also real that God's grace is even greater than that. I have by God's grace kept close relationships with very dear people, people who believed in me when I didn't believe in myself, people who were grateful for me when I thought I was nothing more than damaged goods.

People who remind me of God's grace in Jesus. You need those people in your life, or if you don't you probably will.

My gratitude journey has been a journey with friends: a former colleague who won't let me give up on myself; a former golf buddy and an old neighbor who both check on me and remind me they are grateful for me, an evangelist friend I once did youth camps with, a couple of former students; the list goes on and on. And there is my sweet elderly mom, the most generous person I've ever met, who loves me unconditionally.

More recently I have a new friend with whom I almost daily share something for which I am grateful. I start my day journaling my gratitude and I end my day telling another person something for which I'm grateful. Bookending a day with gratitude is better when someone comes along for the ride and really enjoys the journey.

Putting Gratitude Into Practice

1. Try a Thankful Thursday with your family. Each Thursday as you gather for dinner take time to give specific thanks. Try giving a specific reason to be grateful to God for something, for a person outside the family, and a family member.

2. Find people in your workplace, neighborhood, or other social gathering you can meet with (face to face or online) for a gratitude date to relate specific things you are grateful for.

3. If you are part of a small group at your church, whenever you have a time of prayer, ask to have a specific time to encourage one another by noting your gratitude.

4. For married couples, try the George Bailey effect. Remember George Bailey from *It's a Wonderful Life*? On the edge of taking his life, Bailey remembered how precious the things in his life really are and became thankful.

5. GRATEFUL PEOPLE DEVELOP A LIFESTYLE OF GRATITUDE

"CULTIVATE THE HABIT OF BEING GRATEFUL FOR EVERY GOOD THING THAT COMES TO YOU, AND TO GIVE THANKS CONTINU- OUSLY." — RALPH WALDO EMERSON[50]

"WHEN IT COMES TO LIFE THE CRITICAL THING IS WHETHER YOU TAKE THINGS FOR GRANTED OR TAKE THEM WITH GRATITUDE."— G.K. CHESTERTON[51]

"I DO NOT CEASE TO GIVE THANKS FOR YOU." –– THE APOSTLE PAUL, EPHESIANS 1:16

T im Ferris is one of the more enigmatic authors I've read. His books, including *The 4-Hour Workweek, The 4-Hour Body,* and collections of interviews in *Tools of Titans* and *Tribe of Mentors,* sometimes inspire me and at other times make me scratch my head. He helps me think.

In his book *Tools of Titans* Ferris interviewed an interest- ing collection of people from bodybuilder/actor/politician Ar- nold Schwarzenegger to chef/TV Personality Andrew Zimmern, from Tony Robbins to Seth Godin. He discovered 80 percent of the people interviewed have a daily routine of meditation/mind- fulness practice. He also notes throughout the book examples of routines various people employed.

Ferris personally makes a big deal of morning routines, which

I've found to be helpful for years. Here's his typical day:
#1—Make Your Bed [to] accomplish the first task of the day. Even in hotels.
#2—Meditate (10 to 20 minutes)
#3—Do 5 to 10 Reps of Something (< 1 minute)
#4—Prepare "Titanium Tea"
#5—Morning Pages or 5-Minute Journal (5 to 10 minutes)[52]

He starts his journal by writing three topics of gratitude. He is not a follower of Jesus, yet he has learned what many have missed: the importance of gratitude. How much more should we who have tasted and seen that the Lord is good practice gratitude?

Routines

About 40 percent of what we do daily is habit. One of the best ways to develop good habits is by observing daily routines, especially in the morning when we first get up. Here's a typical weekday for me (understanding I work remotely).

--Make my bed
--Make coffee (and do 10 air squats while it brews)
--Get my Bible and journal
--Open my journal. I currently use a three-ring binder with several tabs. The *first* tab is my gratitude journal, so I write three things for which I'm grateful at the start. The *second* tab is my normal journal where I write what is happening in my life, prayer requests, and things the Lord is teaching me. The *third* tab is for Bible study, where I write what I see in the Word. The *fourth* tab: affirmations (this one I do occasionally and not daily--see Chapter 6). Finally, the *fifth* tab: fitness goals, weight, and any ideas that come to mind.

--I then write on an index card my plan for the day with work. After that I either workout immediately or work a couple of hours and then do my workout.

I also practice the 16:8 Intermittent Fasting approach, eating in an eight-hour window from about 930-530 each day. There's nothing special about my routine except for two things: one, I have a daily routine that's almost automatic. Second, gratitude is central to my routine. Though it takes very little time, it has brought about such a remarkable change.

The Power Of Practice

Brené Brown admitted her research challenged her view that knowledge was more important than practice when it comes to change. "In fact," she said, "It's safe to say that reluctantly recognizing the importance of practice sparked my 2007 Breakdown Spiritual Awakening."[53]

While she believes it's important to have an "attitude of gratitude," she found people who practice gratitude as a routine do so in a variety of ways that fit who they are. Some kept gratitude journals, others offered daily prayers of gratitude, or created works of art expressing gratitude, or in moments of stress stopping to say out loud, "I am grateful for...."

Brown summarized, "It seems that gratitude without practice may be a little like faith without works—it's not alive."[54]

Malcolm Gladwell in his book *Outliers* made famous the "10,000" rule, the idea that those who have put in around 10,000 hours of deliberate practice become experts in their field. He gives the interesting example of the Beatles, who spent time in Hamburg, Germany, playing music eight hours a day many days over a period of a few years before they stormed the rock and roll world and rewrote the history of music.

It's a fascinating study not terribly relevant to our subject except for this: the more you practice gratitude, the more you find it becoming a part of who you are. If gratitude isn't already a daily part of your life, try it for a while. And it doesn't take 10,000 hours to get there. Just writing daily something for which you are grateful over a 21-day period can set you on a path of consistent gratitude. And, there is potency in consistency.

Paul's Practice Of Gratitude

At the start of the chapter, I gave an example of Paul giving thanks to those he wrote. Here's a more complete list:

"I thank my God through Jesus Christ for all of you" (Romans 1:8)

"I give thanks to my God always for you" (1 Corinthians 1:4)

"I do not cease to give thanks for you" (Eph. 1:16)

"I thank my God in all my remembrance of you;" (Philippians 1:3)

"We always thank God" (Colossians 1:3)

"I thank my God always when I remember you" (Philemon 1:4)

"We also thank God constantly" (1 Thess. 2:13)

"We ought always to give thanks to God" (2 Thess. 1:3)

"I thank God whom I serve" (2 Timothy 1:3)

Paul started most of his letters with thanks. He did so even when he addressed a troubled church (Corinth), and while he suffered in prison for his faith (Ephesians, Philippians, Colossians).

Jesus had a habit of gratitude as well. He gave thanks to the Father just after condemning the unrepentant cities of Chorazin and Bethsaida and just before inviting those who were weary to come to Him for rest (Matthew 11:20-30). He gave thanks each time He fed the multitude (Matthew 15:36; John 6:11). He thanked the Father for hearing Him just before He raised Lazarus from the dead (John 11:41), and at the last supper (Luke 22:19). Giving thanks was a pattern in the life of Jesus and in the letters of Paul. May it be of us as well.

Make It A Habit

Developing good habits and stopping bad habits is a topic for another book, but I do want to focus on the simple addition of the helpful habit of gratitude. The simplest way to do this is with a little formula called "When I _____, I will _____." This applies to a lot of things.

For instance, every morning when my keurig is dispensing my coffee I do 10 air squats. Why? Because I told myself, "When I brew my coffee, I will do air squats."

I used to lose my keys. Do you ever do that? When I started saying, "When I walk in the door, I will put my keys in the bowl," losing my keys went away.

Let's apply this simple tool to gratitude. Here are two ways.

Example One: "When I _____ I will give thanks."

--When I sit down to eat, I will give thanks for the food.
--When I meet a friend, I will tell them I'm grateful to see them.
--When I send an email, I will add a statement about something for which I'm grateful.

Example Two: "When I _____ I will write 3 things for which I'm grateful."

--When I get my first cup of coffee in the morning, I will write three statements of gratitude in my journal.
--When I lay down at night, I will write three things from my day I'm grateful for.

In *The Happiness Advantage* Shawn Achor suggests picking the same time each day for your gratitude list and having the items you use ready and available. He gives several examples from his consulting work:

> *When I worked with employees at American Express, I encouraged them to set a Microsoft Outlook alert for 11 A.M. every day to remind themselves to write down their three good things. The bankers I worked with in Hong Kong preferred to write down their list every morning before they checked their e-mail. The CEOs I trained in Africa opted to say three gratitudes at the dinner table with their children each night. It doesn't matter when you do it, as long as you do it on a regular basis.[55]*

It was after my life sunk to the depths that I realized how valuable and real gratitude can be. On my 60th birthday during my season of deep brokenness, my daughter and her husband gave me a gratitude journal. It included a very sweet note from each of them (and a cute scribbling from my then-2-year-old grandson). I used that for several months until it was filled up.

Now as noted above I use a small three ring binder in sections for my journaling. The first section is always gratitude. Whatever your routine, the more you can make it a set, daily habit, the more you will practice it, and the more you will benefit from it.

Make It Creative

The Jar of Awesome/Jar of Gratitude. A friend once gave Tim Ferris a "Jar of Awesome" as a gift. It's simply a mason jar that sits on the kitchen counter so it's hard to miss. The words JAR OF AWESOME are on the side in big letters. Whenever something makes Tim joyful or excited, he writes it on a slip of paper and drops it in the jar.

We try to remember the things that bring us joy and forget things that bring us down. Unfortunately, the opposite usually happens: negative things tend to stick with us while the blessings tend to vanish from our mind's eye. Try using a JAR OF GRATI-TUDE to keep a record of blessings for those tough days when you aren't feeling particularly grateful or joyful.

"It sounds ridiculous to admit," Ferris writes, "but—man—it works. I keep the jar where I will see it constantly. . . . I came to realize that A) If you're serious all the time, you'll wear out before the truly serious stuff gets done; and B) if you don't regularly appreciate the small wins, you will never appreciate the big wins."[56]

The 10-Second Wish. Chade-Meng Tan is a Google pioneer and best-selling author. He encourages people to do a simple exercise:

In many of my public talks, I guide a very simple 10-second exercise. I tell the audience members to each identify two human beings in the room and just think, 'I wish for this person to be happy, and I wish for that person to be happy.' That is it. I remind them to not do or say anything, just think—this is an entirely thinking exercise. The entire exercise is just 10 seconds' worth of thinking. Everybody emerges from this exercise smiling, happier than 10 seconds before. This is the joy of loving-kindness.[57]

Meng gives a specific example of the impact of such a simple, kind act. He did this with a group in California on a Monday night. He also challenged them the next day at work to randomly identify two people in their office and secretly wish happiness for them, once an hour, for only 10 seconds. That's all; no communication with them, just 10 seconds, once an hour, 80 seconds total.

Not long after that training Meng received an email.

"I hate my job," it began. "I hate coming to work every single day. But I attended your talk on Monday, did the homework on Tuesday, and Tuesday was my happiest day in 7 years."

Thinking happy thoughts toward others brings a more grateful spirit to us.[58]

Putting Gratitude Into Practice

Daily Ideas. 1. Get a s gratitude journal. Begin each morning writing three simple things for which you are grateful. Do this at least 21 days in a row.

2. If you keep a regular journal already, start your daily entry with the three things you're grateful for.

3. Set an alert on your phone to stop and give thanks.

Occasional Ideas. 1. Get a *Jar of Gratitude*. Put a pen and index cards or stick-it notes next to it. When you choose gratitude put it in the jar. From time to time to read and reflect on the notes.

2. Write a thank-you note to someone. If possible, deliver it personally; consider reading it to them. You might make this a weekly practice. And, at least once a month write one to yourself.

3. Related to this, purchase a box of thank-you notes. I bought an inexpensive box of assorted notes at a local dollar store that have served me well. Then, when you think of someone you want to send a note you will have them at your convenience.

6. GRATEFUL PEOPLE TURN GRATITUDE TO HOPE THROUGH AFFIRMATIONS

"LET GRATITUDE BE THE PILLOW UPON WHICH YOU KNEEL TO SAY YOUR NIGHTLY PRAYER. AND LET FAITH BE THE BRIDGE YOU BUILD TO OVERCOME EVIL AND WELCOME GOOD."— MAYA ANGELOU[59]

"ONCE YOU BEGIN TO TAKE NOTE OF THE THINGS YOU ARE GRATEFUL FOR, YOU BEGIN TO LOSE SIGHT OF THE THINGS THAT YOU LACK."— GERMANY KENT[60]

"I REMEMBERED THE LORD, AND MY PRAYER CAME TO YOU, . . . I WITH THE VOICE OF THANKSGIVING WILL SACRIFICE TO YOU; WHAT I HAVE VOWED I WILL PAY. SALVATION BELONGS TO THE LORD!" -- JONAH 2:7-9

F itness is an area I've loved most of my life. I enjoy reading about health and fitness as well as listening to podcasts on the subject.

If you are into exercisig and fitness you know the value of compound exercises, those that work multiple muscles groups all at the same time. The squat, deadlift, flat bench press, shoulder press, and row have been called the Big Five of compound exercises. Other exercises (like the bicep curl) are called isolation exercises for obvious reasons: these isolate one muscle as opposed to working many.

If you want to grow spiritually, you know of the big spiritual exercises vital for growth in Christ: Bible study, prayer, corporate worship, sharing your faith, serving others, and being in community (small groups) immediately come to mind. The discipline of gratitude is one we overlook too often.

Gratitude is like a compound spiritual exercise in that it never functions in isolation. Beginning your study of God's Word with gratitude for the ability to study it and the gift it is to us increases our hunger for it. Partnering prayer with gratitude increases our intimacy with God, making prayer more personal. Adding gratitude to community makes relationships sweeter. And, confessing our beliefs with gratitude—the practice I call affirmations—helps to make faith come alive.

In this chapter I want to help you to see the importance of affirmations, declaring truth in order to grow more grateful and build your faith. We all feel inadequate at times in our walk with God; sometimes our life in general feels like a hot mess. In those times, affirming things that are true—regardless of what you've done in the past or how you feel in the moment—can stir both gratitude and faith in moments of doubt.

If you want to be led less by emotion and more by conviction, the practice of declaring affirmations brings clarity in the middle of uncertainty. This can include quoting Scripture, remembering a song declaring truth, or repeating statements of truth so easily forgotten.

Affirmations bring us back to focus on things we often don't see clearly enough. "Grateful living is possible only when we realize that other people and agents do things for us that we cannot do for ourselves," Emmons observed. "Gratitude emerges from two stages of information processing—affirmation and recognition. We affirm the good and credit others with bringing it about."[61]

Gratitude Precedes Action

In the frenetic, pull-yourself-up-by-your-own-bootstraps, workaholic, always-progressing world we live in, the formula for a life of joy or happiness typically goes like this:

Work hard -------> Find joy/happiness

The problem is there are so many workaholics who have sacrificed and worked tirelessly and are still pretty miserable. I meet a lot more people who talk about how weary they are from work than those who find joy in it. A lot of us are really tired. I'm for working hard, but the better order is this:

Gratitude->Joy/Happiness-> Work hard

Gratitude leads to joy and happiness, which motivates people to work hard and to sacrifice. Achor calls this the Happiness Advantage. He notes a study to debunk the "performance leads to well-being" notion:

> *If happiness were just the end result of being successful, the prevailing creed at companies and schools would be correct: Focus on productivity and performance, even to the detriment of our emotional and physical well-being, and we will eventually become more successful, and therefore happier. But thanks to strides in positive psychology, this myth has been debunked. As the authors . . . were able to say conclusively, "study after study shows that happiness precedes important outcomes and indicators of thriving." In short, based on the wealth of data they compiled, they found that happiness causes success and achievement, not the opposite.[62]*

Identifying areas where you struggle mentally, emotionally, or spiritually, and responding with affirmations can have the effect of moving you to gratitude, leading to joy, which contributes positively to your work.

Gratitude leads to joy and happiness, which motivates people to work hard and to sacrifice.

Affirmations As Confessions Of Faith, Not Aligning The Universe

Scott Adams, the creator of the *Dilbert* cartoon, has interesting thoughts on affirmations. His ideas have gotten him into hot water with some of his fans who accuse him (unfairly I think) of treating affirmations almost like magic, which he doesn't actually affirm (sorry). But he has some remarkable anecdotes about his use of affirmations. The most profound practice of affirmations came when he began writing fifteen times daily each morning, "I, Scott Adams, will be a famous cartoonist."[63] That one worked out pretty well.

Adams defines affirmations as "simply the practice of repeating to yourself what you want to achieve while imagining the outcome you want."[64] They can be written, spoken, or thought in sentence form. His simple explanation: "My perception is that affirmations are useful and I have no idea why."[65]

Adams is a very bright fellow (and a compelling writer), but how he uses affirmations is not what I'm talking about. I'm talking more about affirming truth as a confession of faith, which leads to a mindset of gratitude. In the New Testament to "confess" means literally "to say the same thing." So, in Romans 10:9 it says if we confess with our mouth Jesus is Lord, and believe in our heart God raised Him from the dead, we will be saved. Similarly, in 1 John 1:9 we are told if we confess our sins (we agree with God about our sin and don't try to weasel out of it) that God is faithful to forgive.

I'm talking about declaring our faith, not seeking the "Law of Attraction."

I've found that sometimes it's easier for me to encourage someone else with truth from God's Word than to believe it also applies to me. "Sure, nothing can separate us from the love of God," I confidently tell a friend. "But I really screwed up, don't you see?"

I need—and I've found a lot of people need—ruthless attention to familiar truth. We so easily forget what the Bible tells us, especially about grace, because grace runs counter to what we see and experience most of the time.

When I affirm truths about God my soul enjoys gratitude and my faith grows.

Jonah offers a fascinating and surprising example of this. The reluctant prophet's life wasn't marked by gratitude, which is typical for a disobedient disciple like him. God, who is rich in mercy, wanted to offer grace to the Ninevites even though the Assyrian people (Nineveh was the capital of the Assyrian Empire) were ruthless and cruel. Jonah had a hard time grasping God's grace toward sinners, so Jonah refused to be the messenger even though God chose him. Because of Jonah's ongoing obstinacy, God prepared a great fish to swallow him. If you haven't read the book of Jonah, it's a quick read of only four chapters.

God sought to withhold judgment from Nineveh; Jonah refused to deliver hope. Once the fish spat him on the shore, a contrite Jonah offered this affirmation:

When my life was fainting away, I remembered the Lord, and my prayer came to you, into your holy temple. Those who pay regard to vain idols forsake their hope of steadfast love. But I with the voice of thanksgiving will sacrifice to you; what I have vowed I will pay. Salvation belongs to the Lord! (Jonah 2:7-9).

Jonah affirmed the love of God and responded with gratitude. He delivered the message; God showed grace to the Ninevites. Jonah still didn't quite get it (read it yourself to see), but at least for a time he got the point.

We are often like Jonah, wanting to decide who gets the grace of God and who doesn't. That is well above our pay grade. The church today has as many legalists as Jesus faced when He walked on the earth, and I am too often like one myself. But when we grasp the grace and love of God, we not only love others better, we are also able to walk forward by faith.

Personal Affirmations

Affirmations involve the practice of daily or regularly reminding yourself of the things you have been given. How does this not become conceit? By focusing on gratitude. You can state your strengths, your hopes, and your aspirations positively and confidently if they are grounded in gratitude for all God has given.

Affirmations are designed to point us toward the good in a world gone bad. Going over these simple affirmations cause me to be grateful that these things are true.

Often in my journal I will be a little more specific. Early in 2020 I wrote, "I will finish the gratitude book by 11-1-2020." Affirmations like this motivate me to be disciplined.

I often state my affirmations in the form of a prayer.

We can affirm truths that God's Word says about us both as a resource for a grateful attitude and as a reminder of our identity in Christ. Here's an example: most of the time I have pictures of my grandkids as my background on my smartphone. But lately I've listed affirmations for me to see whenever I look at it. I'm finally grasping that I'm more than damaged goods, and that God still has a purpose for me as I walk with Him. I'm prone to forget, so I put these affirmations I believe on my screen:

I am a child of God (John 1:12).
I am a man of God (1 Timothy 6:10).
I am a writer; I will write for the glory of God and the good of others.
I am healthy. I will take good care of myself.
I will serve God's purpose in my generation (Acts 13:36).

The last statement is from King David. Paul said he "served the Lord in his generation" in that passage in Acts. Though David sinned greatly, he is remembered as a man after God's heart who served the Lord. I like to affirm this regularly.

Affirmations bring me back to gratitude which in turn increases my faith. There have been times my faith has been small. Can you relate? Daily and consistently recording my gratitude for the truths about God and His grace toward me over time has grown my faith in unprecedented ways. Today, my faith is stronger than ever, my joy runs deeper, and I find myself more free from the lures of this world and the unhelpful opinions of others. Gratitude started this process as I reflected on Who God is and how He loves me. From desperate brokenness I have found a deep faith.

In this practice I follow one of my great heroes mentioned previously: King David. David never really had it easy. He was overlooked as king at by the great spiritual leader Samuel. He fought the Philistines––including a very famous Goliath––for years. He served a passive-aggressive king named Saul who loved him one minute and wanted to kill him the next.

When David was king, he committed adultery, murder, and tried to cover it up, until the prophet Nathan confronted him. He was later chased away from the throne by his own son Absalom.

Yet, at the end of his life, we have his song. And how did David begin his song? With an affirmation of truth:

The Lord is my rock and my fortress and my deliverer, my God,
my rock, in whom I take refuge, my shield, and the horn of my

salvation, my stronghold and my refuge, my savior; you save me from violence (2 Samuel 22:2-3).

And, it ends with an affirmation of praise and thanksgiving:

For this I will praise you, O Lord, among the nations,
and sing praises to your name.
Great salvation he brings to his king,
and shows steadfast love to his anointed,
to David and his offspring forever (2 Samuel 22:50-51).

Putting Gratitude Into Practice

1. State an affirmation about your identity that is true regardless of how you feel. Look at 1 Peter 2:9 and Romans 8:31 for examples. Take a moment to be grateful for truths that aren't dependent on your feelings.

2. For the next week or so, when you look at yourself in the mirror first thing in the morning, say something affirming to yourself each day, and be grateful.

7. GRATEFUL PEOPLE UNDERSTAND GRATITUDE AS THE PATHWAY TO JOY

"WHAT SEPARATES PRIVILEGE FROM ENTITLEMENT IS GRATITUDE."
— BRENÉ BROWN[66]

"FEELING GRATITUDE AND NOT EXPRESSING IT IS LIKE WRAPPING A PRESENT AND NOT GIVING IT."— WILLIAM ARTHUR WARD[67]

"REJOICE IN THE LORD ALWAYS; AGAIN I WILL SAY, REJOICE. . . .

DO NOT BE ANXIOUS ABOUT ANYTHING, BUT IN EVERYTHING BY PRAYER AND SUPPLICATION WITH THANKSGIVING LET YOUR RE-QUESTS BE MADE KNOWN TO GOD." — THE APOSTLE PAUL, PHILIP-PIANS 4:4, 6

The United States is a world power with more wealth than any other nation including all of Europe combined. But our immense wealth does not seem to be able to buy happiness. Barry Schwartz observed how the "happiness quotient" of Americans has declined over the past three decades even while the GDP or gross domestic product (measuring prosperity) has more than doubled in the same span.[68]

We see evidence of this anecdotally just by reading or watching the news or scrolling through social media. There are a lot of unhappy campers out there today. If wealth is not the key to open the door to happiness or its deeper cousin joy, what is that key?

The key to the door of joy is unlocked not with gold but with gratitude.

In Nehemiah 12, after a long struggle rebuilding the walls of Jerusalem, the people gathered: "And at the dedication of the wall of Jerusalem they sought the Levites in all their places, to bring them to Jerusalem to celebrate the dedication with gladness, with thanksgivings and with singing, with cymbals, harps, and lyres" (Nehemiah 12:27).

What was the effect of their thanksgiving? "And they offered great sacrifices that day and rejoiced, for God had made them rejoice with great joy; the women and children also rejoiced. And the joy of Jerusalem was heard far away" (Nehemiah 12:43). Thanksgiving led to joy.

When I found myself a few years back lying on the floor, weeping over my sin, my failure, my unfaithfulness, and my brokenness, I had no hope but in the Lord. I found that He is enough. Over time, as my lament moved me toward hope in the God who delights in the return of prodigals (Luke 15), I began ever so slowly to rediscover the peace of God. I recall vividly a moment while delivering auto parts. Alone in the truck I found myself thanking God for peace. But I also remember telling my small group leader at his home one day how I now had peace, but not joy.

Gratitude, over time, moved me back to joy, because gratitude took my gaze from my plight to God's might. His glory became central in my praise, and he restored the joy of my salvation (Psalm 51:12). The work of Jesus for me became much more real than my failed efforts for Him. For me personally, gratitude opened my heart to joy. And it can do the same for you.

"One of the most profound changes in my life happened when I got my head around the relationship between gratitude and joy," Brené Brown wrote. She found three patterns in her research:

Without exception, every person I interviewed who described living a joyful life or who described themselves as joyful, actively practiced gratitude and attributed their joyfulness to their gratitude practice.

Both joy and gratitude were described as spiritual practices that were bound to a belief in human interconnectedness and a power greater than us.

People were quick to point out the differences between happiness and joy as the difference between a human emotion that's connected to circumstances and a spiritual way of engaging with the world that's connected to practicing gratitude.[69]

Joy Is More Than Happiness

I want to pick up on Brown's observation on the difference between happiness and joy. Barbara Fredrickson is a researcher at the University of North Carolina and is considered by many to be the world's leading expert on the subject of positive emotions. She prefers the term "positive emotion" to "happiness" because the latter is less focused. Fredrickson listed the ten most common positive emotions. Note the first two highlighted in her list: *"joy, gratitude,* serenity, interest, hope, pride, amusement, inspiration, awe, and love."[70]

What's the difference between joy and happiness? They are both to be desired. But pretty much everyone understands they aren't the same. Happiness tends to be tied to circumstances and is a more surface response to a benefit or blessing. In fact, the term "happiness" comes from "happenstance" which is tied directly to circumstances. Joy is deeper, something less dependent on circumstances and more a mark of one's faith and character.

For years I've understood this, yet in the darkest times joy seemed elusive. Until I found the link between gratitude and joy. I can't fake myself out and choose joy when I'm struggling, but I *can* choose to be grateful. And that triggers joy. Brown agrees:

> *The research has taught me that happiness and joy are different experiences. In the interviews, people would often say something like, "Being grateful and joyful doesn't mean that I'm happy all of the time." On many occasions I would delve deeper into those types of statements by asking, "What does it look like when you're joyful and grateful, but not happy?" The answers were all similar: Happiness is tied to circumstance and joyfulness is tied to spirit and gratitude.*
>
> *I also learned that neither joy nor happiness is constant; no one feels happy all of the time or joyful all of the time. Both experiences come and go. Happiness is attached to external situations and events and seems to ebb and flow as those circumstances come and go. Joy seems to be constantly tethered to our hearts by spirit and gratitude. But our actual experiences of joy—these intense feelings of deep spiritual connection and pleasure—seize us in a very vulnerable way.[71]*

Brown goes on to stress the importance of both. She encourages the practice of recognizing the experiences that make us happy and to create those when we can.

One of the most profound changes in my life happened when I got my head around the relationship between gratitude and joy.—Brené Brown

For instance, I love sitting at a coffee shop catching up with a dear friend. I just did that today, in fact. I love to sit out on the farm in the glider facing the pasture with my laptop, writing in the beauty of God's creation. I also enjoy weightlifting and bike riding. And, I enjoy carpentry work. I try to do all of these with regularity as they bring me happiness. I agree with Brown's thoughts here. First, "In my own life, I'd like to experience more happiness, but I want to live from a place of gratitude and joy."[72]

As I read Brown's words it makes total sense to me why we're a nation hungry for more joy: We are generally an ungrateful and entitled people. She describes a specific practice to show how gratitude helps turn fear into joy: "When I'm flooded with fear and scarcity, I try to call forward joy and sufficiency by acknowledging the fear, then transforming it into gratitude. I say this out loud: 'I'm feeling vulnerable. That's okay. I'm so grateful for _____.' Doing this has absolutely increased my capacity for joy."[73]

Grace, Gratitude, And Joy

Paul's letter to the Philippians is known for its emphasis on joy. In four short chapters he mentions the term in some form 16 times. Paul shows the linkage between grace, gratitude, and joy as he opens the letter: "**Grace** to you and peace from God our Father and the Lord Jesus Christ. I **thank** my God in all my remembrance of you, always in every prayer of mine for you all making my prayer with **joy**" (Philippians 1:2-4).

You can see in Paul's writings the relationship between grace, gratitude, and joy: receiving *grace* evokes the response of *gratitude*, which opens the path to *joy*.

As long as thanks is possible, joy is possible. --Ann Voskamp

Ann Voskamp explains this feature in her powerful book *The Broken Way*. She notes the connection often in the New Testament between the word for "grace" (*charis*), "thanksgiving" (eu*charis*teo), and "joy" (*chara*). This is seen clearly as Jesus instituted Communion:

> *"And he took bread, gave thanks and broke it, and gave it to them..."*

I had first read it slowly, years ago—how in the original language "gave thanks" reads eucharisteo. *The root word of* eucharisteo *is* charis, *meaning "grace." Jesus took the bread and saw it as grace and gave thanks.*

There was more. Eucharisteo, *thanksgiving, also holds the Greek word* chara, *meaning "joy." Joy. And that was what the quest for more has always been about—that which Augustine claimed, "Without exception . . . all try their hardest to reach the same goal, that is, joy."*

Deep chara *is found only at the table of the* euCHARisteo— *the table of thanksgiving.*

I had sat there long . . . wondering . . . is it that simple? Is the height of my chara *joy dependent on the depths of my* eucharisteo *thanks?*

So then as long as thanks was possible, then joy was always possible. The holy grail of joy was not in some exotic location or some emotional mountain peak experience. The joy wonder could be here, in the messy, piercing ache of now. The only place we need see before we die is this place of seeing God, here and now.

I'd whispered it out loud, let the tongue feel these sounds, the ear hear their truth.

Charis. Grace. Eucharisteo. *Thanksgiving.* Chara. *Joy.*

A triplet of stars to reveal the outline of the fullest life, thanksgiving, joy.[74]

Grateful Prayer Overcomes Anxiety

My senior year in college I had to write a paper for my hermeneutics class. Hermeneutics has to do with how we understand and interpret the Bible. I don't recall how the process worked in choosing our passage other than students had some latitude in the choice; what I do know is I chose Philippians 4:6-7. Why that passage? Perhaps even then I was somewhat aware of my issues with anxiety and depression, I'm not really sure. I know this passage has been very dear to me all my life:

> *Do not be anxious about anything, but in everything by prayer and supplication with thanksgiving let your requests be made known to God. And the peace of God, which surpasses all understanding, will guard your hearts and your minds in Christ Jesus.*

We're told not to be anxious. But Paul does more: he gives an alternative. Instead of being anxious, pray. But don't just pray; pray specifically—"let your requests" means very particular prayers. And don't just pray specifically; pray "with thanksgiving." Paul writes this in such a way to state that you aren't really praying unless thanksgiving is in the middle of these prayers. Thanksgiving to God is a form of prayer, after all.

For Paul, the remedy for anxiety is to (1) pause, (2) pivot to prayer, (3) in the middle of that prayer be grateful, and (4) to look away from yourself and your circumstances to the God who hears and helps. Get your gaze fixed on God and only glance at your needs. And what is the promise? God's peace will guard our hearts. Philippi was near the northern border of the Roman Empire. A Roman garrison was there at all times, protecting the city from the barbarians to the north. As the Roman army protects you from harm physically, Paul is saying, God will protect your hearts emotionally and mentally, so you need not be anxious.

Putting Gratitude Into Practice

Robert Emmons encourages people to take time to meditate on what he calls the three small stones: joy, grace, and love. You can see the direct relationship between gratitude and joy in this focus. These three are tangible reminders of gratitude:[75]

1. Joy—look for the good. "Gratitude is the gateway to joy."

2. Grace—receive the good. "Grace, by showcasing the goodness of the giver, helps us to keep our priorities straight."

3. Love—give back the good. "The motivation for giving back the good resides in the grateful appreciation that we have lived by the grace of others."

A practical exercise: think of the next time you will interact with someone in the service industry, such as a server in a restaurant. Plan to give a little beyond the obligatory tip. Make it a point to thank the service for something specific they did. Reach out to their supervisor to praise the server. Spread joy. Related to this, I often ask the server if I can pray for him or her about anything. No one has ever been offended by this; most by far are grateful, even thrilled. Some have broken into tears of gratitude for the simple act of kindness. Gratitude and joy are wonderful companions.

8. GRATEFUL PEOPLE FOCUS ON WHOLEHEARTEDNESS OVER REGRET

"GRATITUDE HAS FITTINGLY BEEN REFERRED TO AS THE QUINTES-SENTIAL POSITIVE TRAIT, THE AMPLIFIER OF GOODNESS IN ONE-SELF, THE WORLD, AND OTHERS, AND AS HAVING UNIQUE ABILITY TO HEAL, ENERGIZE, AND CHANGE LIVES." –– ROBERT A. EMMONS[76]

"TO YOU, O GOD OF MY FATHERS, I GIVE THANKS AND PRAISE, FOR YOU HAVE GIVEN ME WISDOM AND MIGHT, AND HAVE NOW MADE KNOWN TO ME WHAT WE ASKED OF YOU, FOR YOU HAVE MADE KNOWN TO US THE KING'S MATTER." –– DANIEL 2:23

I've had a number of surgeries that required rehab. I break things: I've had both knees repaired and got a complete hip replacement, to name a few. I also injured my back once and was in chronic pain for about a year. I know the desire to have my body feel whole again; I also understand the key role rehab plays when things get broken. Because of that, I have great admiration for physical therapists. One doesn't immediately heal from a broken body or a broken life. For the body, a good PT is crucial to becoming whole.

A PT like Murray.

One season of life I went to three back doctors, took shots, and considered surgery due to chronic pain in my lumbar spine. I went to a chiropractor for a while. Nothing seemed to help. Then, I found Murray. Murray is an Australian who relocated to the U.S. He's also a Physical Therapist specializing in the lumbar spine. He became my PT during my back issues. And he changed my life physically. He taught me some things, showed me stretches and exercises, and within a couple of months I was feeling great. Today I have no back issues.

Sometimes we need outside intervention and expertise to help us overcome the misfortune of a broken body. The same is true of a broken life. For a broken body a PT is most helpful. For a broken life the Scriptures and the Spirit bring healing, along with gracious friends who walk with you on the journey.

Choosing Wholeheartedness

I've been all over the world. I took my daughter in her youth to shop at H&M on four continents (we were there for mission work, not to shop, but shopping also happened). I've traveled across Europe with my son. I've had Starbucks in ten countries and visited a lot more. Seeing the world is great. But to enjoy whole-heartedness in the whirl of everyday life, that is pure joy.

All of us want to be whole. We may define that differently. We may have no idea what it looks like. But we know when we don't have it, and we long for it.

One of the reasons I enjoy reading Brené Brown is her down-to-earth honesty:

I'll fess up about how I became the middle-aged, recovering, health-conscious, creative, touchy-feely spirituality-seeker who spends days contemplating things like grace, love, gratitude, creativity, authenticity, and is happier than I imagined possible. I'll call it Whole-hearted.[77]

Wholeheartedness living, Brown says, "means cultivating the courage, compassion, and connection to wake up in the morning and think, No matter what gets done and how much is left undone, I am enough."[78]

She is talking about identity. I would say it a bit differently. According to the Scriptures I am enough for one reason, and that is because Christ is enough. What He did for broken people like me is enough. What He accomplished on the cross is enough. I could not make myself whole; on my own I totally screwed up my life. But He did everything required for me to be whole.

This is why Romans 8 has become so dear to me. Romans 8:1 declares the unchanging truth that because of Christ there is no condemnation: "There is therefore now *no condemnation* for those who are in Christ Jesus." Romans 8 is rich with the grace of God, which is why I'm writing a four-week devotional on Romans 8 just now. The chapter begins with no *condemnation* and concludes with no *separation*:

> For I am sure that neither death nor life, nor angels nor rulers, nor things present nor things to come, nor powers, nor height nor depth, nor anything else in all creation, will be able to separate us from the love of God in Christ Jesus our Lord (Romans 8:38-39).

It matters what God says about you. And he says, you are enough *in Christ.* That is the beauty of the good news, and why gratitude should be our ever-present disposition. We experience guilt over what we've done; Jesus took our guilt on the cross (as Paul describes in Romans 1-3). We feel the weight of shame because of who we are. In Christ, I have a new identity.

I often *feel* like I am not who God says I am. I don't always *act* as I am in Christ. But I am who God says I am in Christ, period. And that is a reason for thanks!

No Regrets

The opposite of a wholehearted life is a life of regret. We all have regrets. We can't change the past. We can't summon Tony Stark to help us figure out a way to go back in the past and fix things *Avenger: End Game* style. But gratitude can help us to see God's grace even in past regrets; more than that, a grateful life can help free us from a pattern of regret moving forward.

A year or so ago I read Bronnie Ware's book *The Top Five Regrets of the Dying*. Ware spent years in Australia doing palliative care, working with and caring for the dying. Her book reflects on the biggest regrets she heard:

1. "I wish I'd had the courage to live a life true to myself, not the life others expected of me."

2. "I wish I hadn't worked so hard."

3. "I wish I'd had the courage to express my feelings."

4. "I wish I had stayed in touch with my friends."

5. "I wish that I had let myself be happier."[79]

I would like to add: I wish I'd read these carefully about 25 years ago. Now that I'm in my "last third" of life, starting over in many ways, I can see how I failed at all of these to some degree. What about you?

Today I realize so many things I thought brought satisfaction, joy, happiness, and fulfillment––things leading to wholehearted-ness––were either an illusion or unnecessary. I still want to make an impact for the gospel; I want to encourage others. I want to help broken people see hope in Christ.

But I'm far more aware of how God works in the simple things as well as in bigger things, and in broken people. I see Him as much in a newborn calf running across the pasture. I see Him in the kindness of a friend. He shows His glory in many ways, and they are often easily missed.

You don't come to wholeheartedness based on your title or your extra hours at work. You don't get there trying to please other people who don't walk in wholeheartedness themselves. You don't have to perform at a certain level or receive certain recognition. You do need to love God and love people and exchange the temptation to perform with gratitude for what you've already received.

I'm grateful for so many simple things like the fact that I love to write. Maybe I'm not great at it, but it brings me great joy. It has helped a few folks, and that's enough. I'm grateful for my health. I'm the only 61-year-old I know who takes no prescription medicine. I'm in better shape today than when I was 40, and I'm far more at peace.

What I am, more than I've been in a very long time, is content. And that's worth more than my weight in gold.

And for that I am grateful.

Daniel: Wholeheartedness In Tough Times

When you read the first chapter of the book of Daniel you find young Hebrew men in trouble. Babylonian king Nebuchadnezzar's army besieged Jerusalem, resulting in the captivity of Daniel and his companions.

Ripped away from home and everything familiar, being indoctrinated in the foreign beliefs of a foreign people in a foreign land, Daniel faced a reality that doesn't sound like wholehearted living. How did Daniel respond?

He pitched a fit and began to yell at God for being so mean. He was a teenager, after all! No, he didn't. Here's what he did: "But

Daniel resolved that he would not defile himself with the king's food, or with the wine that he drank. Therefore he asked the chief of the eunuchs to allow him not to defile himself" (Daniel 1:8). He honored God, and God blessed him. The story is fascinating and it's well worth your time to read both Daniel 1 and 2, but in a nutshell, God gave Daniel the ability to interpret dreams, which he did for the king in Daniel 2. Daniel's service to the king meant he and his companions were spared death.

It's hard to live a wholehearted life when you are dead, right? This is why Daniel, rather than being frustrated by his captivity and the circumstances of life sought to honor God no matter what. As a result, Daniel proclaimed:

Blessed be the name of God forever and ever, to whom belong wisdom and might. He changes times and seasons; he removes kings and sets up kings; he gives wisdom to the wise and knowledge to those who have understanding; he reveals deep and hidden things; he knows what is in the darkness, and the light dwells with him. To you, O God of my fathers, I give thanks and praise, for you have given me wisdom and might, and have now made known to me what we asked of you, for you have made known to us the king's matter (Daniel 2:20-23).

What is true for Daniel in his faithfulness to God is available to God's children even when we fail Him, which is why the good news in Jesus is so very good. "When we sin and mess up our lives," Peterson says, "we find that God doesn't go off and leave us—he enters into our trouble and saves us. That is good, an instance of what the Bible calls gospel."[80] He adds how to put this into practice: "we can act ourselves into a new way of feeling much quicker than we can feel ourselves into a new way of acting."[81]

This ties directly into the practice of gratitude. Choosing to pause to be grateful can lead us into a more wholehearted life; waiting for circumstances (or the universe, or whatever) to grant us wholeheartedness mystically is not the path born out either by research or by Scripture.

A joyful life of grace toward others grows
best in the soil of gratitude. —Paul Tripp

The reality of the grace of God is the circumstance we need to pursue wholeheartedness. Turia Pitt reminds us: "The Earth doesn't stop spinning just because you made a mistake."[82]

Paul Tripp states the reality for the follower of Christ: "There really is nothing that we will ever need to admit to and to honestly face that hasn't been fully addressed by the grace that is ours because of the life, death, and resurrection of Jesus." In case we still don't get this, he adds, "There is nothing that we could ever do that is outside that grace."[83]

That's why we sing "amazing" grace.

Set Free From People Pleasing

We have to figure out what keeps us from wholeheartedness. This involves being curious, seeking God in prayer, and getting counsel from godly friends. I have been a chronic people pleaser most of my life (I bet I'm not the only one). I finally realize I no longer have to please people; I just want to please the Lord.

In the process of growth in recent days I came to a revelation. It's pretty simple, and thus it shows how thick-headed and slow to learn I can be. The revelation is this: in my life, almost 100% of the anxiety I've experienced (and it's been a lot), much of my depression, and far too many of my decisions—including stupid and sinful choices —have been a *direct result* of the fear of man in my life. When I took time to reflect on this, it was quite startling.

The response to this has not been to ignore relationships; instead, I've learned to depend much more on God's Word and a small circle of trusted friends who love me unconditionally and care for me enough to offer both correction and encouragement. It is hard to put into words how freeing this has become.

Be the person God made you to be. Don't be more, don't be less. If you screw up, you don't have to give up. He won't.

As followers of Jesus we have nothing to prove; we only have Someone to please.

Choosing to be grateful in the middle of brokenness and hurt provides a light to help you look up from the shadows of your pain. Being grateful doesn't ignore pain and problems, but it looks at them with curiosity, turning the issue back to the Lord to find something gracious in the middle of it.

We don't need to act like something that is not good is good; we can be honest about reality. After all, you can't face reality with gratitude if you don't look at things honestly.

Gratitude can't take away the suffering in our lives, but it helps with our perspective toward it. The apostle Paul understood suffering to be part and parcel of life. We live in a day of escapism and denial; Paul said to face suffering as a gift: "For it has been granted to you that for the sake of Christ you should not only believe in him but also suffer for his sake" (Philippians 1:29).

This is not some form of spiritual masochism or a resignation to a hard life, but a recognition that even in suffering we can learn valuable lessons, and how we suffer can bring glory to God.

Putting Gratitude Into Practice

1. Take time each night to think about the blessings of the day. Give thanks for those.

2. If you have a habit of waking up during the night or sleep restlessly, try turning to gratitude in those times you lie awake. Instead of counting sheep, try counting blessings.

3. Think about an area of your life that has brought pain. Can you think of ways to be grateful even in the midst of that pain? Not by denying the hurt, but by seeing something gracious in the middle of it.

CONCLUSION

"I WAITED PATIENTLY FOR THE LORD; HE INCLINED TO ME AND HEARD MY CRY. HE DREW ME UP FROM THE PIT OF DESTRUCTION, OUT OF THE MIRY BOG, AND SET MY FEET UPON A ROCK, MAKING MY STEPS SECURE. HE PUT A NEW SONG IN MY MOUTH, A SONG OF PRAISE TO OUR GOD. MANY WILL SEE AND FEAR, AND PUT THEIR TRUST IN THE LORD.

BUT MAY ALL WHO SEEK YOU REJOICE AND BE GLAD IN YOU; MAY THOSE WHO LOVE YOUR SALVATION SAY CONTINUALLY, 'GREAT IS THE LORD!' AS FOR ME, I AM POOR AND NEEDY, BUT THE LORD TAKES THOUGHT FOR ME. YOU ARE MY HELP AND MY DELIVERER; DO NOT DELAY, O MY GOD!" –– KING DAVID, PSALM 40:1-3, 16-17

G ratitude saved my life.

Literally. Or, at least I believe it did.

What do you do when you find yourself in what seems like a hopeless situation? You can choose to run, and there are many paths open for that. Or, drown yourself in bottomless bottles of liquor; or, get your hands on enough pills to numb out.

Or, if those don't work and despair keeps strangling

you, there is the ultimate road: suicide. Just end it all. This is real. It is a way people try to cope.

I once found myself sitting in my driveway in despair, thinking seriously about pulling into the garage, taking a big handful of pills to put me fast asleep, dropping the garage door with the van running and the windows open, and allowing the carbon monoxide to take me away. All my surface success seemed like nothing. I was in my mind a complete failure. The most important relationships in my life were broken. Perhaps the best thing I could do for everyone would be to remove myself from this life. Maybe that would give me peace and end the pain.

But before I opened the bottle or the garage door, I paused. And, I reflected. I thought not about me and the shipwreck of my life; I thought about the love of God and the anchor He had always been. Sitting there, my vehicle changed from a tomb to a temple, filled with the love of a merciful God.

As I sat there, I became grateful. I pictured the real, spiritual, genuine relationship I had with God. I sensed Him tell me He loved me still. It was irrevocable. It was not a mirage. It was real. God's love was still there, even though it had seemed faint just moments before.

I remembered Romans 8:31: *If God is for us, who can be against us?*

Gratitude would not let me go.

I couldn't *not* be grateful.

I recalled I Thessalonians 5:18: "Give thanks in all circumstances; for this is the will of God in Christ Jesus for you." And I gave thanks. Though more heartache would come, I never let go of His grace.

If you read this and still find despair overtaking gratitude, don't give up. I'm so glad I didn't. I'm so grateful today for life, and hope, and peace, and yes, for joy. I found gratitude wouldn't let me go.

I'm not sure how close I came to following-through on my plans as I sat in my driveway that day. Not very, I think now. I know I had come to a place where my trajectory was taking me to a place where self-harm became easier by the day.

I still had my faith. In fact, since the moment of reckoning my faith has steadily grown since. It's amazing how honesty grows faith. The more honest you are with God, the more real he is to you.

I also had a few people, and by a few, I mean enough, who cared for me no matter what. The Bible talks about a unique kind of love called *agape*. It's an unconditional kind of love. It is the love shown by Christ on the cross. It's very rare even in the church today.

And, I had gratitude. I *have* gratitude. It has made all the difference.

If you read this to the end and find yourself still struggling, there is hope. Email me at ALRAdvising@gmail.com. Call a friend or loved one and tell them your hurt. Let's learn together the joy that comes even in the dark through the simple habit of gratitude.

Maybe your life is great right now overall. Perhaps you are in a season of abundance. What more reason to develop the habit of gratitude?

Let's begin each day with gratitude and see what's in store.

The best *is* yet to be.

Notes

[1] *https://kk.org/thetechnium/68-bits-of-unsolicited-advice/*, accessed August 1, 2020.

[2] https://gratefulness.org/grateful-living/moving-from-the-pain-of-addiction-to-living-gratefully/, accessed August 25, 2020.

[3] Ann Voskamp Facebook Page, November 19, 2019.

[4] Robert A. Emmons, *The Little Book of Gratitude* (Octopus Books, Kindle Edition) 7.

[5] Timothy Ferris, *Tribe of Mentors: Short Life Advice from the Best in the World* (Houghton Mifflin Harcourt, Kindle Edition, 16.

[6] https://azdailysun.com/flaglive/cover_story/mind-over-matter-no-excuses-for-mountaineer-kyle-maynard/article_79239542-dc09-54f3-9b70-b05043a700d2.html, accessed May 17, 2020.

[7] Emmons, *Little Book of Gratitude*, 86.

[8]   https://www.canr.msu.edu/news/gratitude_part_1_what_is_it_and_how_do_i_include_it_in_my_life, accessed May 17, 2020.

[9] Ed Stetzer, *Christians in the Age of Outrage* (Tyndale, 2018).

[10] Emmons, *Little Book of Gratitude*, 7.

[11] Ibid., 7-8. Emphasis added.

[12]   https://www.telegraph.co.uk/books/what-to-read/winnie-the-pooh---aa-milnes-winnie-the-pooh-characters-in-quotes/piglet-noticed-that-even-though-he-had-a-very-small-heart-it-cou/, accessed September 17, 2020.

[13] Brennan Manning, *The Ragamuffin Gospel* (Multnomah, 2005), 89.

[14] Timothy Ferriss, *Tools of Titans: The Tactics, Routines, and Habits of Billionaires, Icons, and World-Class Performers* (Houghton Mifflin Harcourt. Kindle Edition), 319.

[15] Ibid.

[16]   https://relevantmagazine.com/culture/14-maya-angelou-quotes-about-living-life-purpose/, accessed September 17, 2020.

[17] Ferris, *Tools of Titans*, 399.

[18] Brennan Manning, *The Ragamuffin Gospel* (Multnomah, 2005), 80-81.

[19] Emmons, *Little Book of Gratitude*, 10.

[20] Ibid.

[21] Ibid., 81.

[22] Shawn Achor, *The Happiness Advantage: How a Positive Brain Fuels Success in Work and Life* (The Crown Publishing Group, Kindle Edition), 97-98.

[23] https://positivepsychology.com/benefits-of-gratitude/, accessed May 21, 2020.

[24]   https://greatergood.berkeley.edu/article/item/how_gratitude_changes_you_and_your_brain, accessed May 25, 2020.

[25] Emmons, *Little Book of Gratitude*, 21.

[26] Ibid., 20.

[27] https://greatergood.berkeley.edu/article/item/why_gratitude_is_good, ac-

cessed August 29, 2020.

[28] Ibid.

[29] https://gratefulness.org/resource/gratitude-motivates-us-become-better-people/, accessed July 22, 2020.

[30] Roy T. Bennett Twitter @InspiringThinkn, August 31, 2017.

[31] http://ciscohouston.com/docs/docs/quotes/bonhoeffer.html, accessed September 17, 2020.

[32] https://www.opendoorsusa.org/christian-persecution/stories/4-things-persecuted-believers-can-teach-us-about-gratitude/, accessed August 3, 2020. Names changed for security reasons.

[33] Shawn Achor, *Big Potential: How Transforming the Pursuit of Success Raises Our Achievement, Happiness, and Well-Being* (Currency, 2018), 17-19.

[34] Ferriss, *Tools of Titans*, 543.

[35] Ibid., 486.

[36] Ibid., 314.

[37] Ibid., 404.

[38] Ibid.

[39] C.S. Lewis, *The Four Loves* (Harvest Books, 1971), 78.

[40] Paul David Tripp, *New Morning Mercies* (Crossway. Kindle Edition), 537.

[41] Tim Ferris, *Tribe of Mentors: Short Life Advice from the Best in the World* (Houghton Mifflin Harcourt, Kindle Edition), 98.

[42] Greg Mckeown, *Essentialism: The Disciplined Pursuit of Less* (The Crown Publishing Group, Kindle Edition), 197.

[43] https://positivepsychology.com/benefits-of-gratitude/, accessed May 21, 2020.

[44] Ferriss, *Tribe of* Mentors, 35.

[45] Shawn Achor, *Before Happiness: The 5 Hidden Keys to Achieving Success, Spreading Happiness, and Sustaining Positive Change* (Currency, Kindle Edition), 54.

[46] Ann Voskamp, *The Broken Way* (Zondervan. Kindle Edition), 268.

[47] Chris Crowley and Harry S. Lodge. *Younger Next Year: Live Strong, Fit, and Sexy - Until You're 80 and Beyond* (Workman Publishing Company. Kindle Edition), 257).

[48] From https://www.health.harvard.edu/healthbeat/giving-thanks-can-make-you-happier:, accessed May 8, 2020.

[49] Chris Crowley and Jen Sacheck, *Thinner This Year: A Younger Next Year Book* (Workman Publishing Company, Kindle Edition), 66.

[50] https://leadx.org/articles/we-know-we-ought-to-be-grateful-but/, accessed September 17, 2020.

[51] https://www.thegospelcoalition.org/blogs/justin-taylor/5-quotes-from-g-k-chesterton-on-gratitude-and-thanksgiving/, accessed September 17, 2020.

[52] Ferriss, *Tools of Titans*, 146-147.

[53] Brené Brown, *The Gifts of Imperfection: Let Go of Who You Think You're Supposed to Be and Embrace Who You Are* (Hazelden Publishing, Kindle Edition), 78.

[54] Ibid., 79.

[55] Achor, *The Happiness Advantage*, 102.

[56] Ferriss, *Tools of Titans*, 570.

[57] Ibid., 157-158.

[58] Ibid., 164.

[59] https://www.goalcast.com/2017/08/17/10-maya-angelou-quotes-to-give-you-backbone-in-times-of-struggle/

[60] https://zunews.com/2020/03/zu-magazine-seeing-vs-perceiving-the-world-of-social-media/

[61] Emmons, *Little Book of Gratitude*, 14.

[62] Achor, *The Happiness Advantage* 41-42.

[63] Scott Adams, *How to Fail at Almost Everything and Still Win Big: Kind of the Story of My Life* (Penguin: Kindle Edition), 44.

[64] Ibid., 154.

[65] Ibid., 155.

[66] https://www.amazon.com/What-separates-privilege-entitlement-gratitude/dp/1655325566

[67] https://www.amazon.com/dp/1655327399/ref=rdr_ext_tmb

[68] Barry Schwartz, *The Paradox of Choice* (Harper Collins, Inc., Kindle Edition), 201.

[69] Brown, *Gifts of Imperfection*, 77-78.

[70] Achor, *Happiness Advantage*, 40.

[71] Brown, *The Gifts of Imperfection*, 45.

[72] Ibid., 80.

[73] Ibid., 84.

[74] Voskamp, *The Broken Way*, 29.

[75] Emmons, *Little Book of* Gratitude, 67-72.

[76] Ibid., 21.

[77] Brown, *The Gifts of Imperfection*, xiv.

[78] Ibid., 1.

[79] Bronnie Ware, *The Top Five Regrets of the Dying* (Balboa Press, 2011), Kindle Edition.

[80] Eugene H. Peterson, *A Long Obedience in the Same Direction: Discipleship in an Instant Society* (IVP Books, Kindle Edition), loc 665.

[81] Ibid.

[82] Ferriss, *Tribe of Mentors*, 169.

[83] Tripp, *New Morning Mercies*, 531.

ABOUT THE AUTHOR

Alvin Reid

Alvin "Al" Reid has enjoyed the wonderful highs and the devastating lows of life. This journey taught Al both a greater appreciation of grace and a deeper compassion for the outcast, the broken, and the marginalized.

He writes full time now, copywriting, editing, and writing for others as well as his own books and resources.

He does this all from the family farm in the rolling hills of north Alabama where he helps his mom daily. He also loves time with his kids and their families, particularly his grandkids he loves so dearly, and close friends. For interviews, speaking invitations, information, or other services you can reach him at alradvising@gmail.com or www.beinspiredbooks.com.

BOOKS IN THIS SERIES

The RE Series

The prefix "RE" comes from a Latin term meeaning "back to the original place." This series calls for a return to those things often overlooed, forgotten, or in need of change. These short, practical books in most cases will also include small group resources.

Books in the series will include:
RESTORING GRATITUDE: Finding Beauty in a Broken World
REVOLUTIONARY GRACE: A 28 Day Devotional on Romans 8
RETHINING THE MISSION: Life As a Mission Trip
REDEEMING TIME
REVITALIZE THE CHURCH
RESCUING HABITS
REORIENTING DISCIPLESHIP

Restoring Gratitude

Made in the USA
Columbia, SC
17 November 2020